Murdo A.N. Macleod

Bible Truth
Explored

REFORMATION
SCOTLAND

Contents

The Lord's prayer: Questions 99-107

Preface

All the way through Scripture we find an emphasis on teaching-particularly to the young, the ways of truth. Each generation is to praise God's works to the next and to declare the mighty acts He has done. The way the Church has often done this in the past, particularly in times of difficulty, is by catechising. They teach the basics of sound doctrine by means of question and answer.

The Westminster Shorter Catechism is one of the most used and best loved ways of teaching Bible Truth so, by learning its contents, we are taught what we are to believe and what is required of us by the Lord. Once these truths are fixed in the mind they are not easily forgotten and can prove to be a help and a bulwark in later years.

Some might dispute the value of teaching young people matters which they do not always readily understand. The Bible assures us, however, that if we "Train up a child in the way he should go: and when he is old, he will not depart from it" (Proverbs 22:6). Indeed, if we neglect train up our children, we can be assured that the world will certainly not hesitate to do it!

The added advantage of catechising is that we also learn what we do not believe: error is identified and we can be on our guard. In this way, we are all better protected against the danger of false teaching and heresy damaging or even derailing our walk with the Lord. In these days of spiritual confusion, we need a straightforward guide to biblical truth.

Bible Truth Explored began as a series of articles in the Explorer Magazine, a monthly magazine for young people published by the Free Church of Scotland (Continuing). These articles have been significantly revised and edited to form the chapters of this book. I am deeply grateful to those who have contributed so much to reshaping and editing the content, particularly Catherine Hyde together with Matthew and Janet Vogan. This book is now sent out to a wider public with the prayer that the Lord would be pleased to use it for His own glory.

Murdo Angus Macleod

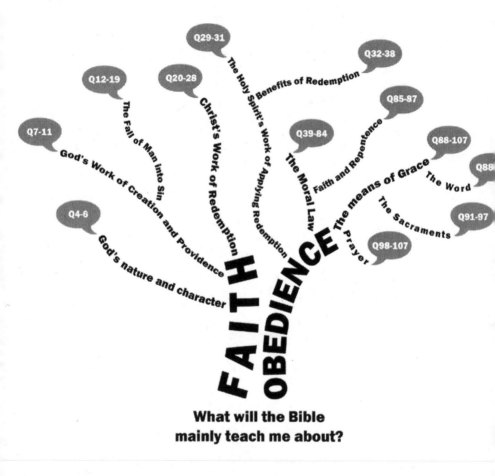

**What will the Bible
mainly teach me about?**

What is a Catechism?

A catechism summarises the Bible's teachings through questions and answers. The question and answer format allows the truths to be presented in an organised way and makes the truths easier to learn and remember.

When was the Shorter Catechism written? The Shorter Catechism was produced by a gathering of ministers and theologians called the Westminster Assembly. This assembly met in London in the seventeenth century. They produced a clear statement of the Christian faith, known as the Westminster Confession of Faith. They also agreed biblical principles on matters of worship and how the church should be run. They published two catechisms, the Larger Catechism and the Shorter Catechism, in 1648.

What is in the Shorter Catechism? The Shorter Catechism consists of 107 questions. It has three main parts. The first part is introductory and consists of Questions 1 to 3. The second part, from Question 4 to 38, tells us what we are to believe. The third part, from Question 39 to 107, tells us what we are to do.

Why learn the Shorter Catechism?

It helps us summarise Bible truth. The Shorter Catechism is very short. It only includes the most essential doctrines. It covers the key truths about God, creation and providence, how we fell into sin, and God's way of saving sinners. It also unpacks God's requirements for how we should live our lives, and explains what we must do to be saved. It also opens up what we must do to be saved and explains God's requirements for how we should live our lives. Much (but not all) of the teaching in the Westminster Confession is condensed into the Shorter Catechism. It gives us what we need to grasp first of all.

It helps us remember Bible truth. Generations of believers, with their children, have not only read the Shorter Catechism but memorised it. By learning it off by heart, we fix its important truths in our mind so that we can use it again and again and so that it shapes our thinking and our behaviour.

It helps us defend Bible truth. By its brief and precise wording, the Shorter Catechism gives us a ready-made articulation of what the Bible teaches. We don't have to start from scratch or use our own words every time we want to explain some part of Christian doctrine. Instead we can use the descriptions and definitions which are carefully crafted, ready and waiting in the Catechism.

> "The Shorter Catechism gives us a ready-made articulation of what the Bible teaches."

It helps us learn Bible truth. In the Catechism we learn about the most important subjects, such as who God is, what He has done to save us from our sin and how we should obey God through keeping His commandments. It teaches us about this life, and life after death. It also helps us understand about the Trinity and the ways God communicates His grace. We can learn the Catechism ourselves by reading and answering the questions.

What is the purpose of life?

Why did God make me? What is the purpose of life? Why am I here? These are important questions that most people ask at some point in their lives. The Shorter Catechism dives in at the deep end by tackling this fundamental issue in the very first question. "What is man's chief end?" is basically asking, "What is the point of our existence?"

> 💬 What is the chief end of man?
>
> Man's chief end is to glorify God, and to enjoy him forever.

No special purpose?

Many people think that we have no special purpose in life. They think everyone can choose their own goals in life, because there is no more to life than enjoying ourselves and getting the most out of our time here. What a poor, selfish attitude that is! Jesus told us about a man who said to himself, *"Take thine ease, eat, drink, and be merry"* (Luke 12:19). Because that was his sole purpose in life, God called him a fool. The Catechism tells us that we do have a purpose, or an *"end,"* a goal or aim in life.

Many special purposes?

Many people also think that there are many special purposes for living. They include to work and look after our families, education, science and development, and of course recreation. While all these are important in their own place, none of them is our chief end. We have one *"chief"* purpose, one special, supreme aim. Glorifying God is not just the whole point of our existence it is the over-ruling purpose for everything that exists.

To glorify God

Our chief end has two aspects. The first aspect is *"to glorify God."* Does this mean that we have to try and make God more glorious than

"We have one 'chief' purpose, one supreme aim."

He already is? No. We cannot add to God's glory. It is already perfect. It can neither be increased nor reduced.

However, there can be variation in how God's creatures display His glory. Think of the sun. We cannot make the sun shine brighter, but clouds sometimes hide or block the sun's brightness. We cannot make God any more glorious than He is. But our sins are like clouds, which hide or overshadow God's glory. Our sins make the world a darker place and obscure God's honour.

To *"glorify God"* is not to add to His glory but to live in such a way as honours Him and declares His gloriousness to all who see and hear us. It is to live a life of obedience to God, not hiding His glory behinds clouds of disobedience.

Our duty is to do everything to the glory of God. Our lives are not divided into parts, one part about spiritual matters and the other part worldly concerns. It is not a case of having one part of our lives obeying God and another driven by a desire to please and glorify ourselves. Whether at home or work, study or leisure, our whole lives are to be focused on glorifying God.

To enjoy God

"Enjoying God means being pleased and delighted with who God is."

The other aspect of our chief end is **"to enjoy God for ever."** Enjoying God means being pleased and delighted with who God is, finding Him to be the one source of our deepest satisfaction and pleasure. This enjoyment is a consequence of glorifying God, although it should not be our main motivation for glorifying God. We should glorify God because God is so glorious, not because of the pleasure we may consequently experience.

When we think of how we enjoy God, we can think both of enjoying Him in this world and of enjoying Him in the world to come.

Enjoying God in **this world**
The Christian enjoys the presence of God. This is because God has restored a friendly relationship between Him and them. Instead of being afraid of God and antagonistic towards Him, the Christian finds pleasure and satisfaction in the presence of God.
The Christian enjoys pleasing God. Instead of making it their priority to please themselves, or keep other people happy, the Christian enjoys thinking about God and how they can serve Him and glorify Him best with their lives and talents.
The Christian enjoys activities in which they meet with God. Instead of being most happy when God is pushed to the back of their minds and feels very far away, the Christian enjoys every opportunity to spend time with God. These opportunities include reading the Bible, praying, and worshiping church services on the Lord's day.

Enjoying God in **the world to come**
The Christian's enjoyment will last **"for ever"** because God is everlasting. The enjoyment of God which the believer has in this world is only a little foretaste of what they will enjoy in eternity. In heaven, they will be able to completely and continually glorify and enjoy God.

Our chief end is something that should absorb our attention and energy. It should never be far from our thoughts that the main reason for our existence is to glorify and enjoy God. When we are more concerned about our own glory, and find our pleasures in other things, we show that we are not fit for our main purpose and our priorities are all wrong. We should take Paul's advice, **"Whether therefore ye eat, or drink, or whatsoever ye do, do all to the glory of God"** (1 Corinthians 10:31).

⚲ Something to think about...

- What does it mean to glorify God, since it is impossible for us to make God any more glorious than He is?
- Life is pointless without an ultimate purpose. Some people find the Bible negative because it tells them about their sin but isn't their idea of a meaningless world governed by chance the most negative?

Personal reflection
If you were write a list of *'Things I Enjoy,'* would you include God? If not, what needs to change?

What is the only guide for life?

In Question 1 we saw that our chief purpose is to glorify God and enjoy Him for ever. But how do we go about fulfilling this purpose? How will we know what to do? Question 2 explains that God has told us what we need to know.

> 💬 What rule hath God given to direct us how we may glorify and enjoy him?
>
> The Word of God, which is contained in the scriptures of the Old and New Testaments, is the only rule to direct us how we may glorify and enjoy him.

God has given **His Word**

God has given us our reason and our conscience. From these we have some sense of moral right and wrong and some ability to work out what God is likely to be pleased with. This is sometimes called 'the light of nature.' God also displays His glory in creation and arranges things in providence so that we can get some idea of what angers Him and what He finds acceptable.

> "In His Word God communicates to us what we need to know in order to achieve our chief end."

This is sometimes called 'general revelation.' But neither the light of nature nor general revelation – nor both combined – is an adequate source of information as to how we may glorify and enjoy God.

Instead, God has given us His Word. This is sometimes called 'special revelation.' We have *"the Word of God,"* a revelation from God Himself, in words that humans can understand. In His Word God communicates to us what we need to know in order to achieve our chief end. Obviously, God's Word does not include everything that is possible to be known. But what it does include is everything that is necessary to be known for salvation – what we should believe and how we should behave.

God has contained **His Word**

God has spoken at various times in long ago history through prophets, and by dreams, visions and audible voices. But now He has given us His Word in writing. He has collected up everything He wants us to know, and compiled it into the Bible. God's revelation of everything we need to know is not scattered around in multiple locations. He has *"contained"* it for us inside the scope of *"the scriptures of the Old and New Testaments."*

When the Catechism says that the Word of God *"is contained in the Scriptures,"* it does not mean that the Scriptures include some content we can call God's Word alongside other content which is not God's Word. All of Scripture is God's Word. Nor does it mean that the Scriptures consist merely of written words which become the divine Word of God when we receive it. Scripture is the divine Word of God whether or not we receive it as such. Instead, to say that the Word of God *"is contained in the Scriptures"* means that the whole of God's special revelation is confined to the Scriptures. We won't find God's revelation of how He wants us to glorify and enjoy Him anywhere other than the Scriptures.

God directs us only by His Word

The Scriptures are *"the only rule"* which God has provided to direct us on the question of glorifying and enjoying Him. A 'rule' in this sense is the ultimate authoritative standard. Of course it is appropriate to refer to secondary, subordinate rules, such as the Westminster Confession of Faith and indeed the Shorter Catechism itself. We can also use the help of theologians, philosophers, historians, linguists, ethicists, scientists, and others to understand what we should believe and do. But these other sources are all subservient to the Scriptures and we should respect them only to the extent that they are true to Scripture. Our ultimate authority is always the Scriptures.

"Our ultimate authority is always the Scriptures."

Our only rule is *"the Scriptures of the Old and New Testaments."* The 39 books of the Old Testament and the 27 books of the New Testament are what constitute the Scriptures, the Word of God. All and only these 66 books are the Word of God.

God uses His Word *"to direct us."* This was God's purpose in giving us the Scriptures, and He designed the Scriptures to be exactly what we need. Because these are God's words, they come with all God's authority, all God's truthfulness, and all God's accuracy. Because God is not only true but also faithful, He has provided us with a revelation that can be understood. Although not every part of Scripture is equally easy to understand, yet Scripture is sufficiently clear that ordinary people who read it straightforwardly are capable of grasping its main messages.

So, if we want to know how to fulfil our chief end, what we need to do is consult the Scriptures. The Scriptures are exactly what God wants us to know in order to glorify and enjoy Him, they are entirely reliable, and they are to be simply accepted and reverently obeyed.

Q Something to think about...

- Where can we hear the Word of God speaking today, other than in Scripture?
- How far should we follow our conscience as a guide to right and wrong? How far should we follow the customs of our godly forefathers as a guide to how we should behave?
- What features of the Scriptures make them fully adequate to be our only rule to direct us?

Personal reflection
Read Psalm 119:24. What is your response to God's Word?

What are the Bible's main teachings?

God's Word is our authority to direct us how we are to glorify and enjoy Him. What then is the main content of God's Word? Question 3 highlights the two main areas of teaching in Scripture: what we are to believe about God, and how we should live. In other words, the main teachings of the Bible are about faith and action. Question 3 sets the scene for all the remainder of the Shorter Catechism. The Catechism will expand on 'what we are to believe' in Questions 4 to 38. Then it will cover 'what we are to do' in Questions 39 to 107.

💬 What do the scriptures principally teach?

The scriptures principally teach what man is to believe concerning God, and what duty God requires of man.

What we are to believe

The Bible was not given to teach us everything we could ever learn in this world. It does not tell us all about all the details of our daily lives. It is not meant to give us a complete history of everything that has ever happened in the world. That is not its purpose. It is given to teach *"what we are to believe concerning God."*

"Without the Bible we cannot find out what we need to know about God for salvation."

What we believe matters

Some people may say that it does not matter what you believe so long as you have faith of some kind. The Bible never encourages this way of thinking. God's Word states clearly and often that it alone is the truth. It shows us the only way to God. The Lord Jesus said, *"I am the way, the truth, and the life: no man cometh unto the Father but by me"* (John 14:6). We must know what we should believe. The Bible tells us what this is.

What we are to believe about God

The Bible tells us what we are to believe about God. Question 4 goes on to tell us what God is like. We need the Bible in order to believe this. Although creation tells us of God's power (Psalm 19:1), it does not tell us about salvation from sin.

Without the Bible we cannot find out what we need to know about God for salvation. Without it, we would be ignorant about God's mercy and grace in Christ. We would know nothing of how and why the Lord Jesus came into the world. Without the Bible how could we know clearly about heaven and hell and how sinners may be saved?

How we are to live

How should we live? Some people say we do not need to worry about this, we should just live as we like. This goes against the teaching of the Bible. It is not enough to know what we are to believe; we must also obey what the Bible tells us.

We are to obey God because He is our Creator and also our Ruler. He has an absolute right to demand our obedience and we have no right to disobey Him.

As we read the Bible we see that it has very clear instructions on how we are to live our lives. No matter how old or important we are, its rules are the same. It speaks to parents and children, to rulers and ordinary people, to rich and poor.

The Bible tells us that above all else we need to repent and believe, turning from our sin and trusting in the Lord Jesus Christ as our Saviour.

> "The Bible tells us that above all else we need to repent and believe, turning from our sin and trusting in the Lord Jesus Christ as our Saviour."

⌕ Something to think about...

- What are the two main areas of teaching in Scripture? (2 Timothy 1:13)
- Does it matter what exactly you believe, as long as you have faith of some kind?
- Can you list a few places in the Bible where we are given very clear instructions on how we are to live our lives?

Personal reflection
The answer to this question provides the structure for the whole of the Catechism. Does it provide the structure for the way that you live your life?

What is God like?

What is God? What is God like? This is one of the most important questions any of us can ever ask. In the previous chapters we have already begun to answer these questions. We have seen that God created us to glorify and enjoy Him. We have also seen that He is a God who has spoken to us through His Word. Question 4 will now take us much deeper into the nature and character of God.

> 💬 What is God?
>
> God is a Spirit, infinite, eternal, and unchangeable, in his being, wisdom, power, holiness, justice, goodness and truth.

God is a **Spirit**

When Jesus spoke to the woman of Samaria He reminded her that *"God is a spirit"* (John 4:24). When we say that God is a spirit, this means that He does not have a physical body and He cannot be seen or touched. A spirit is also rational (or intelligent) and personal. When the Bible refers to God as a spirit, it additionally means that God is living, in the sense that He has life in Himself and is the source of life for everything else in existence.

Angels are spirits. Our souls are also spirits, in the sense that they are not physical, they are rational, and they are personal. But unlike all other spirits, God is not dependent on anyone or anything else for His existence. He is infinite, whereas all other spirits are finite. And whereas other spirits are personal, God is three persons, as we will see in more detail when we come to Question 6.

1. Unique aspects of God's being

Question 5 lists three aspects of God's being that are unique to Him: **Infinite, Eternal and Unchangeable.** These are aspects that no other being can have. Even in heaven believers and angels will never have these characteristics. They are sometimes called God's incommunicable attributes.

2. Shared aspects of God's being

This question also lists seven aspects of God's being that angels and humans may have: being (or existence), wisdom, power, holiness, justice, goodness, and truth. These are often called God's communicable attributes because we share them in a lesser way - not infinitely, eternally, and unchangeably, but finitely, constrained by time, and variably. God is completely and perfectly wise, good, powerful and so on. By contrast, our being is finite, our wisdom is limited, our power is dependent. Our holiness, justice, goodness, and truth are sometimes more conspicuous by their absence, whereas God would cease to be God if He did not possess these attributes in a complete and perfect way.

> "God ... has life in Himself and is the source of life for everything else in existence."

God is **infinite**

Infinite means without measure, bounds or limits. This means God is limitless and totally immeasurable. Our souls are spirits but they are certainly not infinite. The angels are spirits but they are not infinite: they are contained in a particular location. But this is not the case with God (Job 11:7-9). He is present everywhere and therefore asks *"Do not I fill heaven and earth?"* (Jeremiah 23:24).

God is **eternal**

The angels, glorious as they are, had a beginning and of course we all had a beginning. God is eternal: He exists continually, has neither beginning nor end and He is not constrained by time. Psalm 90:2 states that He is from everlasting to everlasting and existed before the world was created.

> "God ... is independent of everything and everyone. No one made God; no one gave Him being."

God is **unchangeable**

We know that we are very changeable. The world we live in and everything in it changes and we change along with it. Our knowledge, understanding and habits are always changing. We also know that the angels are changeable. God, however, is absolutely unchangeable. He is *"the Father of lights with whom is no variableness, neither shadow of turning"* (James 1:17).

God is

God exists. Nothing can be added to His being, and nothing can be taken away. We, of course, also have a being but our being is dependent on God for everything. We would not exist if God had not created our first parents and given us being. God, on the other hand, is independent of everything and everyone. No one made God; no one gave Him being.

God is **altogether wise**

Our wisdom is very limited and is at best imperfect. God's wisdom is an unlimited and perfect wisdom. We see this wisdom most clearly in creation, providence and redemption.

In creation we see how well, how wisely and how perfectly the world was made. Genesis 1:31 says, *"God saw everything that he had made, and, behold, it was very good."* What blindness not to see the evidence of the Creator in the universe! The house you live in did not appear by itself or by accident. Someone designed it and built it. Who else but such a God as is revealed in His Word could have designed this universe of ours?

We also see the wisdom of God in His providence. This is the wise way in which He rules and orders events in the world. It is true that the wisdom of God in providence is not always immediately obvious but we can rest assured that what He does is always wise.

The wisdom of God shines even more brightly in His plan and work of redemption. Only divine wisdom could have devised such a work of salvation, in which God is *"just, and the justifier of him which believeth in Jesus"* (Romans 3:26).

God is **altogether powerful**

Even the most powerful person in the world has limited power for a limited time. The Bible makes clear to us that God is all-powerful (or omnipotent). The Lord said to Abraham that he need not fear any enemies because his God was the **"Almighty God"** (Genesis 17:1). He proved Himself to be so to Abraham and every subsequent generation of His people.

They are **"kept by the power of God through faith unto salvation ready to be revealed in the last time"** (1 Peter 1:5). God uses His omnipotence for His own glory and for the good of His church. By this power He will, at last, destroy Satan and all his works. It is a solemn thing to realise that this power will ultimately be exercised in the salvation or damnation of each individual.

"Our wisdom is very limited and is at best imperfect. God's wisdom is an unlimited and perfect wisdom. We see this wisdom most clearly in creation, providence and redemption."

"God's nature is completely pure. His name is holy ... He can never stop being anything other than completely holy."

God is **altogether holy**

God's nature is completely pure. His name is holy (Psalm 111:9). He can never stop being anything other than completely holy. Each of the three persons of the Godhead is holy (John 17:11, Romans 14:17, Acts 4:27). All His works are holy (Psalm 145:17). Not even the holy angels are holy as God is holy. They cry out **"Holy, holy, holy"** (Revelation 4:8).

God is **altogether just**

People often complain of a lack of justice, and despair of finding justice in this world. But God is infinitely just and righteous both in himself and in all his dealings with his creatures. The justice of God is seen in Christ being punished for the sins of His people as their substitute (Isaiah 53:5). It is also seen in the punishment of all unbelievers for their own sins on the day of judgment (2 Thessalonians 1:7-9). All sin must be dealt with because of God's justice. It will either be dealt with through the blood of Christ or eternal punishment. We can depend on the justice of God: He will always punish sin and reward good.

God is **altogether good**

God is altogether good in Himself and He is the author of all good. The Psalmist says of God, **"Thou art good, and doest good"** (Psalm 119:68).

Even in a sin-ruined world there are many examples of God's goodness. His goodness appears in all that He created (Genesis 1:31). It is seen in His patience towards the wicked (Romans 2:4). Most especially we see the goodness of God in saving undeserving sinners.

God is **altogether true**

We live in a world where many lies are told and many are deceived. Satan is described as a liar, and the father of lies (John 8:44). God, however, is truth and He is the truth itself. God's truth appears in His Word. There is no falsehood, no mistakes, no exaggeration; indeed the Bible tells us that it is impossible for God to lie (Hebrews 6:18).

We can rely on God's Word - every promise and every warning is absolute truth. God's truth and faithfulness will be displayed in the greatest way at the day of judgment. Rewards and punishments will be given as He has foretold in the Scriptures.

Q Something to think about...

- What does it mean when we say that God is a spirit?
- What three aspects of God's being are unique to Himself?
- What aspects of God's being does He share (to some extent) with His creatures?

Personal reflection
This part of the Catechism describes a being who is utterly glorious. Does this match your understanding of what and who God is?

How many Gods are there?

Question 5 is short and easy to learn. However the subject here is one that calls for careful consideration. We have to avoid the temptation to repeat it without thinking about it. It is essential that we have the right answer to this question because ignorance in this area will lead us to dangerous error and idolatry.

> **5** Are there more Gods than one?
>
> There is but One only, the living and true God.

Why is it **important?**

"The true God has spoken to us the truth in His Word."

It was important **in Bible times**

When Israel was in the land of Egypt they would have seen the Egyptians worshipping many idols. Not only did they not worship Jehovah but they had a great variety of gods. We call this polytheism. When the Israelites entered Canaan they were again amongst polytheists who believed in all sorts of false gods.

The Lord teaches Israel very clearly that this was wrong. In Deuteronomy 6:4 we read, **"Hear O Israel: The LORD our God is one LORD."** We find the same message in the New Testament. The Apostle Paul says, **"there is but one God"** (1 Corinthians 8:6). It is estimated that at the time Paul wrote these words, the Greeks had some thirty thousand gods!

It is important **today**

There are still many polytheists in the world. For instance Hinduism is polytheistic. Many people would say that we are free to worship any god and any number of gods we wish. They do not like being told that there is only one God. Nor do they wish to hear that there is only one way to heaven and only one Saviour, the Lord Jesus Christ.

God is **the living God**

One thing that all false gods have in common is that they have no life. In Psalm 115 we read that they have mouths, eyes and ears but they cannot speak, see or hear. Unlike all false gods, **"The Lord is the true God ... the gods that have not made the heavens and the earth, shall even they perish from the earth, and from under these heavens. "They are vanity, and the work of errors."** (Jeremiah 10:11, 15).

This is a part of the lesson that Elijah taught the Israelites on Mount Carmel (1 Kings 18). He said that if the idol Baal was really a living god he would hear and send fire on the altar that his prophets had prepared. All day the prophets called on Baal but, of course, no fire came. But Elijah called on the living God, who immediately answered his prayer.

The living God is also the source of all life (Acts 17:28). He gives life to all His creatures and by His power He preserves all living things. He is also the one who gives eternal life to all who repent of their sins and come to trust in Him as Saviour.

God is **the true God**

God is the true God as opposed to all false idols. Jeremiah, preaching to the people of his own day said, **"the LORD is the true God"** (Jeremiah 10:10). The true God has spoken to us the truth in His Word. That is why it is so important that we read and obey His Word.

○ **Something to think about...**

- Some people would never dream of worshipping a false god such as Allah or a Hindu deity. But anything can become an additional, false god if it competes for more of our time, attention and love than we give the true God - even people or things. What are the main competitors against God in our culture?
- When people say they are atheists, the reason they often give is based on a misunderstanding or a misrepresentation of who God really is. If they knew *the living and true God,'* could anyone remain an atheist?

Personal reflection
Have you come to believe and trust in the one living and true God?

What is the Trinity?

If you have seen a baptism you may have noticed what the minister said as he administered the baptism. He would have baptised the person in "the name of the Father, and of the Son, and of the Holy Ghost." These three persons, the Father, the Son and the Holy Spirit, are what we call the Trinity. Question 6 teaches us about the Trinity.

> How many persons are there in the Godhead?
>
> There are three persons in the Godhead; the Father, the Son, and the Holy Ghost; and these three are one God, the same in substance, equal in power and glory.

God the **Father**

Throughout Scripture the Father is spoken of as God. *"God the Father"* is a common expression throughout the New Testament (e.g., Romans 15:6, 1 Corinthians 8:6, 1 Peter 1:2). No one who takes the Bible at all seriously will doubt that the Father is God, as He is spoken of as having all the characteristics of God, performing all the works of God, and being worshipped as God. In the Gospels Jesus spoke many times of God the Father. It was the Father who sent Him into the world and He returned to the Father when His work in the world was completed.

God the **Son**

Clearly the Father is God. However, there is more than one person who is regarded and worshipped as God. There is also God the Son, a distinct person from the Father, who is equal in power and glory with the Father. *"The Word was with God and the Word was God"* (John 1:1). The Son of God is not a created person, as some cults blasphemously teach. As God the Father was from all eternity, so too was the Son,

"All three are all wise, all powerful, all holy and all good."

"Before Abraham was, I am" (John 8:58). An old statement of faith, the Nicene Creed, written in 325 AD, speaks of the Son of God as *"very God of very God,"* that is, really and truly God, lacking nothing of the essence of God.

God the **Holy Spirit**

The Father is God, the Son is God, and one more person is also God: the Holy Spirit. The Bible teaches that the Spirit, while a separate person from the Father and Son, is also God. In Acts 5:4 Peter rebukes Ananias and Sapphira for lying to God, while in verse 3 he says they lied to the Holy Spirit.

The Bible tells us that the Holy Spirit does work that only God can do but has a different function from the Father and the Son. For instance, the Spirit brings people to spiritual life (John 3:5). He also strengthens, helps and teaches His people, as in John 14:16-17: *"I will pray the Father, and he shall give you another Comforter, that he may abide with you for ever; even the Spirit of truth."* This work highlights the distinct nature of the Holy Spirit. The (so-called) Jehovah's Witnesses claim that the Spirit is only a name for the power of God the Father, but as we see from the Bible they are in error here.

Three persons but One God

There are three distinct persons in the Godhead but there is only one God. These three are *"the same in substance."* They share in the same essence: *"There are three that bear record in heaven, the Father, the Word* [that is, the Son]*, and the Holy Ghost: and these three are one"* (1 John 5:7). All three are *"equal in power and glory."* All three are infinite, eternal and unchangeable. All three are all wise, all powerful, all holy and all good.

"There are three distinct persons in the Godhead but there is only one God."

Q Something to think about...

- The Trinity of persons in the one divine essence is an unfathomable mystery. Since we can't understand it, some people respond by rejecting it in unbelief. What would be a better response (or responses) to the doctrine of the trinity?
- Look up the following verses and explain how they show each of the three persons acting as only God can act and/or receiving the worship due only to God.
  (a) Matthew 28:19
  (b) Matthew 3:16-17
  (c) 2 Corinthians 13:14
  (d) 1 Peter 1:1-2
- If someone has been baptised in the name of the Father and of the Son and of the Holy Ghost, (a) how does this set them apart from the followers of every other religion? and (b) how should they think of themselves in relation to God?

What are God's decrees?

Questions 7 and 8 deal with the "decrees" of God, a concept which is very important in understanding how God makes His plan for us and our world and how He puts His plan into action.

7 What are the decrees of God?

The decrees of God are, his eternal purpose, according to the counsel of his will, whereby, for his own glory, he hath foreordained whatsoever comes to pass.

8 How doth God execute his decrees?

God executeth his decrees in the works of creation and providence.

What is a decree?

When Jesus Christ was born, Mary and Joseph had to go to Bethlehem. This was necessary because *"there went out a decree from Caesar Augustus, that all the world should be taxed"* (Luke 2:1). Caesar Augustus had a plan and he, as Emperor, determined that this plan would be carried out.

The Bible tells us that God also has a plan. It is Biblical to speak of the decrees of God; the Lord is a God who *"worketh all things after the counsel of his own will"* (Ephesians 1:11).

"All was planned by Him according to His wisdom and desire."

of our will and the will of others. God however, had neither counsellor nor need of a counsellor. All was planned by Him according to His wisdom and desire (Isaiah 40:12-15).

The Apostle Paul speaks of God acting *"according to his good pleasure which he hath purposed in himself... according to the purpose of him who worketh all things after the counsel of his own will"* (Eph esians 1:9-11).

God's decrees are His alone

We do not know who Caesar Augustus discussed his plans with. Perhaps he had counsellors who helped him as rulers often do. Sometimes we make decisions as a result of having sought advice or having reached an agreement with other people. Often the end result is a combination

God's decrees are eternal

We can plan ahead, but as we do not know what even the next moment will bring, all is very uncertain. But the decrees of God are from all eternity and will certainly come to pass. Before God created anything, He knew what He would create.

He knew what He would do with all He made. *"Known unto God are all his works from the beginning of the world"* (Acts 15:18).

God's decrees **are effective**

God's plan will be carried out perfectly just as He planned. Caesar Augustus did his best to ensure that his plan was carried out exactly as he wished but even Roman Emperors were limited in their powers. But God is unlimited in His power to bring His plans to completion. Nothing that man or devil can do will ever upset these plans. In the book of Daniel it is said of the Lord that *"he doeth according to his will in the army of heaven, and among the inhabitants of the earth: and none can stay his hand, or say unto him, What doest thou?"* (Daniel 4:35). He carried out the work of creation without using anything but the word of His power. In providence, He normally uses means to carry out His plans.

God's decrees **are detailed**

God has decreed *"whatsoever comes to pass,"* that is, everything that happens. His plan includes everything in time and eternity. It includes everything done by people, angels, animals, and inanimate objects, from each individual's birth to death and everything that happens in between. It includes both the final outcome, and the means and processes which contribute to that outcome. Since it includes everything this also includes permitting sinful actions. They are part of God's overall plan but God is not responsible for these sins. They are committed voluntarily by the individual (James 1:13). God cannot sin and does not try to make anyone sin (James 1:14).

God's decrees **are fulfilled**

As Question 8 points out, God does not just have a plan in His mind, He actually *"executes"* His decrees, or puts them into practice. When He does so, everything that happens corresponds exactly to how He planned it. Nothing that happens is outside of God's plan. He works out His plan in the works of creation and providence. We will look at these works in more detail in the following chapters.

God's decrees **are purposeful**

God has planned everything for His own glory. There is no such thing as a purpose that is more important than the glory of God. Because God is who He is, it is only appropriate that everything should be planned for His glory. We cannot always see the reason for why things happen, or the connection between what happens and God's glory. This is because of the limitations of our knowledge and understanding. God's plan, and His plan in action, are not only wise and good, but calculated in every detail to glorify God.

> "God has planned everything for His own glory."

🔍 Something to think about...

- Why did God not need to consult with anyone outside of Himself when He made His plans?
- According to Daniel 4:35, nothing and nobody can thwart God's plan. What kind of person can take comfort from this? What kind of person should worry about this?
- How does creation reflect the nature of God's decrees?

Personal reflection
Do you agree that it's appropriate for everything to be planned for God's glory?

How did everything begin?

Most people, at some point, question how the universe and everything in it came into existence. How do we account for all the great oceans like the Atlantic and the Pacific? Where did all the countries of the world, like the huge land of Australia, come from? What about the mountains like Everest, K2 and even Ben Nevis? An even greater wonder is the sun, the moon and the planets. How did they come to be in the sky? On a winter's night we look up and see all the stars shining and we have the same question: how did they come to be there?

Every day we are bombarded with answers to these questions. Books and newspapers repeatedly tell us it all came about by accident. Television and radio programmes have the same message. In some way or other, we are told, these things just evolved over many billions of years. Many people are confused and deceived.

There is no need for confusion and uncertainty. When we go to the first two chapters of Genesis, we find that God made this great universe. The Bible tells us how everything came into existence.

What is the work of creation?

The work of creation is, God's making all things of nothing, by the word of his power, in the space of six days, and all very good.

God made **everything**

The very first verse in the Bible reminds us that God Himself has always been and that He created all that was made. Before He made the first people, Adam and Eve, He made a world for them to live in. The universe has not always existed nor did it gradually evolve. Atoms did not just come together in some haphazard way but *"In the beginning God created the heaven and the earth"* (Genesis 1:1).

God made **everything out of nothing**

When you build a house, you need bricks and wood. But in creation God did not use any existing materials. There was nothing in existence other than God himself until

> "There was nothing in existence other than God himself until God began to create."

God began to create. He made everything out of nothing.

God made **everything by the word of His power**

Hebrews 11:3 tells us that *"the worlds were framed by the word of God."* Look at Genesis again. *"And God said, Let there be light: and there was light"* (1:3). This sequence is repeated again and again with all that God made. In His infinite power God called into existence what was not there before.

God made **everything out of nothing in six days**

God could have created everything in a moment but in His wisdom he chose to do it over a period of six days, resting on the seventh. This leaves us a pattern and an example of stopping our ordinary work on one day out of seven. It also shows us God's wisdom in following an orderly course of action.

God made **everything very good**

When He had finished creation God surveyed all He had made and saw that it was all very good (Genesis 1:31). There was neither evil or any flaw in all creation. Out of nothing God had made a perfectly ordered universe which revealed the majestic glory of His eternal power, wisdom and goodness.

Amongst the other good things which God had made were a man called Adam and a woman called Eve. In the next chapter we will look specifically at the creation of human beings.

"Out of nothing God had made a perfectly ordered universe which revealed the majestic glory of His eternal power, wisdom and goodness."

Q Something to think about...

- In your opinion, which of the aspects of God's work of creation gives the most reason to praise Him? All things of nothing - by the word of His power - in the space of six days - all very good?
- What features of creation display the glory of God's (a) power, (b) wisdom, and (c) goodness?

Personal reflection
How does the fact that we are God's creatures give us an incentive to honour God?

Who were the first people?

In the previous chapter we considered the wonderful work of creation, in which the power, wisdom and goodness of God are so clearly displayed. Question 10 focusses on just one aspect of creation – the creation of human beings.

What is so special about humans that a whole question is devoted to them? After all, in comparison to the whole universe, Adam and Eve were very small indeed. The Catechism follows the example of the Bible, which pays particular attention to this part of creation.

> **10** How did God create man?
>
> God created man male and female, after his own image, in knowledge, righteousness and holiness, with dominion over the creatures.

What were the first people like?

Physically Adam was made of the dust of the earth. Eve was made out of Adam (Genesis 1:21-22). When we die and our bodies decompose they return to dust. This is another evidence that we were indeed created as Genesis tells us.

As well has having physical bodies, Adam and Eve also had souls. This makes humans unique among God's creatures, as animals have bodies but not souls, and angels are spirits but do not have bodies.

Adam and Eve were like God but, of course, that does not mean that they were the same as God. God was the infinite Creator and they remained his finite creatures. They were made in God's *"own image."* This does not mean that in some outward way they resembled God. God is a spirit and has no body. What it means is that inwardly, in their souls, they were like God. Their soul was like God in being spiritual and immortal with an understanding and will. The Catechism tells us that there are three different aspects to

"They were ... righteous in their wills, happily choosing and purposing only what was perfectly conformed to the will of God."

their being made in the image of God.

They had **knowledge**

God is a God of knowledge and understanding. Humans are able to gain wisdom and understand the world in which they live. Adam was able to give descriptive names to the animals and also to his wife. We are told that he called her Eve because *"she was the mother of all living"* (Genesis 3:20). But humans also know God in a way that no other creature can. They are able to understand the law and will of God. Humans have been made to know God personally and to be in a relationship with Him.

They had **righteousness**

God is just, fair and righteous. Adam and Eve were created with righteousness. They were righteous in the sense of being morally upright and having perfect love to each other. They were also righteous in their wills, happily choosing and purposing only what was perfectly conformed to the will of God.

They had **holiness**

Adam and Eve loved God in every way. They wanted to do what was right because they loved God and what was right and good. They were pure, with no sinful thoughts, words or actions. Holy also means 'set apart for God'. They were dedicated, consecrated and devoted to God, to do His will in a perfect world.

What is the significance of God making them **male and female?**

What makes human beings particularly special is the fact that we have souls, which were made in the image of God. But our bodies are important too. The Catechism notes that God created human beings *"male and female."* Whether someone is male or female is a biological fact. A man cannot become a woman, and a woman cannot become a man.

One man and one woman

At first Adam was alone with just the animals for company, but God had planned something better for Adam. *"And the LORD God said, It is not good that the man should be alone"* (Genesis 2:18). He was given Eve, who could provide companionship in a way that no animal could, for she was a fellow human being.

God made a man and a woman and brought them together in marriage. Not two men or two women, or one man and several women. This is the only pattern God has given for marriage. Therefore, this is the only possible form that marriage can take, no matter what people may say or how our society changes. There are no examples in the Bible, of God approving of homosexual partnerships. Instead such relationships are forbidden (Leviticus 18:22, Romans 1:24-27). Although there are several examples of God's people in polygamous marriages, these were against God's will. We think of Abraham with Sarah and Hagar, or David and Solomon with their many wives. The Bible notes these relationships as historical facts but nowhere commends or encourages it. Polygamy is rather forbidden (Leviticus 18:18). Breaking God's order for marriage by polygamy is not a pattern to copy but a pitfall to avoid. How often we see things going wrong, even for these people in the Bible, when they ignored the God-given rule and pattern.

Male and female

It is worth noting that Eve as well as Adam was made in God's image, in knowledge, righteousness, and holiness. In this way Adam and Eve had more in common with each other than they had differences. Although men and women have different characteristics and abilities, their differences are intrinsically good as God made them. The suitability of the first woman to be a helper for the first man is grounded in her sharing the image of God in the same way as the man.

Although marriage is one special way in which a man and a woman help each other in life, men and women who are not married to each other still share the same Creator, the same chief end, and the same image of God. Men and women need to relate to each other in families and in

"Adam and Eve loved God in every way."

society in more ways than just as marriage partners - for example as brothers and sisters, and neighbours. It is not the case that God wants each man and each woman to be married, as if singleness is inherently inferior to marriage. Men and women are valuable and have valuable roles to fulfil whether they are married or single.

What special role did the first people have?

Adam and Eve were given a special role: to have *"dominion over the creatures." "And God blessed them, and God said unto them, Be fruitful, and multiply, and replenish the earth, and subdue it: and have dominion over the fish of the sea, and over the fowl of the air, and over every living thing that moveth upon the earth"* (Genesis 1:28). They were to govern all the creatures of the world. This gave Adam and Eve the right and the responsibility to work in agriculture, science, technology, art, and every other area which puts the resources of creation to use for the good of human beings.

🔍 Something to think about...

- What is so special about humans?
- Our bodies were made of dust and will eventually return to dust. How should this affect the way we live our lives?
- We all were originally made in God's image. Although we have lost our original righteousness, we still have a soul which was made in the image of God (see Genesis 9:6, Acts 17:28 and James 3:9). How should this help us (a) to love and praise God, and (b) to love and value each other?
- *'Men and women have more in common with each other than differences.'* Do you agree?
- Dominion over the creatures includes making use of the resources of creation for the good of human beings. Does this mean we don't need to care about environmental issues?

Personal reflection
The moral image of God consists of knowledge, righteousness, and holiness. Does it seem desirable to you to resemble God in this way?

How does God still work in creation?

In previous chapters we have considered God's power in creation. The Bible clearly teaches that God continues to look after and oversee all that He made. Scripture makes clear that His power is as necessary to maintain the world as it was to make it (Hebrews 1:3). Some believe that God created everything but then left creation to continue by itself with no continual involvement. But this is not what the Bible teaches (Psalm 103:19).

> 💬 What are God's works of providence?
>
> God's works of providence are, his most holy, wise and powerful preserving and governing all his creatures, and all their actions.

> "The Lord rules and directs all His creatures... just as surely as He preserves them."

God's providence **preserves**

God sustains the whole creation in existence moment by moment, upholding all things by the word of His power (Hebrews 1:3). Psalm 36 states, **"LORDS, thou preservest man and beast."** He does this by constantly providing for them. People sometimes talk about the *'laws of nature,'* often forgetting that it is really the Lord who is providing for His creatures. He constantly provides what is necessary for them to survive and flourish. He controls the seasons, the water cycle, and all the features of ecosystems (Psalm 104). If God ever suspended His preserving work, everything would simply go out of existence. In Psalm 104 and Matthew 6:26-34 you will find more teaching on this topic. God preserves **"all his creatures, and all their actions."** In Him we live and move and have our being (Acts 17:28) . Every breath we take and all our ways belong to Him (Daniel 5:23).

God's providence **governs**

Psalm 66 asserts that, **"He ruleth by his power for ever"** (v.7). The Psalmist was reflecting on the truth that the Lord rules and directs all His creatures and all their actions just as surely as He preserves them. The sun, moon, stars and all celestial bodies are under His hand. The Bible speaks of the wind, rain and snow at His command. Kings, prime ministers and presidents do not reign and govern by chance. It is by His power and authority that they come and go (Proverbs 8:15-16).

God's providence **is holy**

God is holy in all His ways and works. He governs His own creation in holiness and in such a way as will promote holiness. Because we see so much evil and wickedness happening, we can sometimes struggle to see the holiness of God in His providence. For example, the fact that God

governs all the actions of His creatures includes
even the sinful actions of sinful creatures. God is nevertheless still holy and acting in holiness when He permits sinners to have evil thoughts and gives them good health and energy to put wicked ideas into action. At the same time God remains holy. He is not the author of sin and He is not responsible for the sins of sinful beings. His governing in providence includes setting limits on people's wickedness, and limits on the damage their wickedness causes. His holiness can be seen in His mercy, when He brings good outcomes out of sinful actionsgood outcomes out of sinful actions, and when He converts He converts notorious sinners into dear saints. God's holiness can also be seen in His justice, when He brings bad consequences on sinners for their bad actions. For example, the conspirators who wanted innocent Daniel to be destroyed were themselves soon punished by being thrown into the lions' den (Daniel 6:24).

> "His holiness can be seen in His mercy, when He brings good outcomes out of sinful actions."

God's providence **is wise**

Think of the history of Joseph in Genesis. His life was full of sadness and difficulty, but at last it became clear that God had a wise plan in it all and worked it out perfectly. *"But God meant it unto good, to bring to pass, as it is this day, to save much people alive"* (Genesis 50:20). The reason for many things in life may not be clear to us but we are to trust in God's purposes (Romans 8:28). We see

wisdom in action when somebody uses the best tools and methods to reach the best outcome, even when we don't initially understand what they are doing. It might seem strange, for example, to infect people deliberately with cowpox, giving them unpleasant lesions and fever, but once someone has had cowpox they are protected from smallpox, a deadly disease. God is using the best methods even when our limited wisdom prevents us from seeing how His methods will ever achieve a good outcome.

God's providence **is powerful**

Do you remember proud King Nebuchadnezzar? He thought that there was none as important or powerful as he himself. But God humbled him and taught him that the King of Heaven has power beyond any mere men. Nebuchadnezzar put it like this: *"none can stay his hand,"* meaning that no one can interfere with or alter His powerful oversight (Daniel 4:35). When God announced that He was going to set the Israelites free from Egypt, there was nothing that cruel Pharaoh could do to stop them. He might have thought he had survived the plagues which God had sent, and he must have thought the Israelites were at his mercy when his armies cornered them on the brink of the Red Sea. But he was no match for God's power in providence. In preserving, managing, arranging, and governing, God is not only capable but invincible.

Q Something to think about...

- God is constantly in control of all His creatures and all their actions. Can you think of some examples (from the Bible or your own observation) where God demonstrates either His holiness, wisdom, or power as He preserves and governs (a) something tiny, (b) something enormous, (c) a living creature, (d) an inanimate force of nature, (e) a notorious sinner, (f) a godly believer?
- Someone has compared the operation of God's providence to a clock which has lots of cogs and wheels. They may go in opposite directions but they fit together and all work together to make the clock keep time. How can we see this in the life of Joseph?

Personal reflection

How should the fact that God's providence is simultaneously holy, wise, and powerful make us willing to accept whatever happens to us in our lives?

How did God test Adam?

You may have seen pictures showing Adam and Eve, some trees, a piece of fruit (usually an apple) and, of course, a serpent. This is how most people regard the Garden of Eden and all that took place there - just a story or a fable that never really happened; something that has no effect on our lives. But nothing could be further from the truth.

> **12** What special act of providence did God exercise toward man in the estate wherein he was created?
>
> When God had created man, he entered into a covenant of life with him, upon condition of perfect obedience; forbidding him to eat of the tree of the knowledge of good and evil, upon the pain of death.

Real events

The Scriptures tell us that Adam and Eve and what happened in the Garden of Eden are not myths but real historical events. They are just as real as the history of the Second World War, or the sinking of the Titanic. Of course, there are many historical events that have had no great effect on our lives. They are just things that happened long ago in far away places. But when we think about the Garden of Eden, we are dealing with historical events that have had an effect on the lives of everyone who has ever lived. So what did happen in the Garden of Eden that was so important?

Real covenant

In the Garden of Eden, God made an agreement with Adam. This arrangement had all the ingredients of a real covenant. It had persons making the agreement (God and Adam), it had a condition (perfect obedience) and it had consequences (life if the condition was met, otherwise death).

This covenant was a *"special act"* "of God's providence" towards our first parents. God does not owe His creatures anything for their obedience. He had every right to expect perfect obedience from Adam, and nothing required Him to offer Adam any reward for this. Adam was given very special treatment compared to all the rest of creation when God made a

"God does not owe His creatures anything for their obedience."

covenant with him.

Various names are given to this covenant. Here the Catechism calls it the *"covenant of life,"* referring to the life which it promised. It is also often known as *"the covenant of works,"* referring to the *"works"* of perfect obedience which Adam had to perform.

Real test

The condition of the covenant was that Adam had to give God perfect obedience. Specifically, God told Adam and Eve that they were forbidden to eat from a certain tree in the Garden of Eden - the tree of the knowledge of good and evil.

Adam and Eve were sinless. They loved God perfectly and had the ability to obey God perfectly. God told them that they could eat from all the other trees in the garden, so they would not be short of food if they avoided this tree. Everything about Adam, and everything about Adam's circumstances, was favourable to meeting the condition of the covenant.

Yet it was a real test. With all the advantages on his side, would Adam choose to obey God or disobey? Adam had all the resources to make the right choice, and he carried all the responsibility if he made the wrong choice.

> "Adam and Eve were sinless. They loved God perfectly and had the ability to obey God perfectly."

Real consequences

This was a real covenant with a real condition and real consequences. The danger of failure was made completely clear: *"In the day that thou eatest thereof* [from the tree of the knowledge of good and evil], *thou shalt surely die"* (Genesis 2.17).

Death can be thought of in different ways. Natural death is when someone's soul is separated from their body. Spiritual death is when someone loses God's favour and fellowship. Eternal death is when someone is eternally separated from God's favour. All this was really included when God made a covenant with Adam *"upon the pain of death."*

But this was a covenant of life. Death was threatened for breaking the condition, but life was promised for meeting the condition. Adam would have enjoyed all aspects of life if he had obeyed: natural life, always full of energy, and free from illness and pain; spiritual life, always walking in close and loving fellowship with God; eternal life, eternally enjoying the favour of God. All this was really included in the reward when God covenanted with Adam for life.

🔍 Something to think about...

- We have already seen that humans were special in God's creation. Now they get special treatment in the form of a covenant. How should this shape our views of God?
- The covenant of life was not an agreement between equals, but God stooped down by a vast distance when he made a covenant with His creature. What does this tell us about (a) the love of God, (b) the dignity of Adam?
- Was it reasonable for God to require Adam to give perfect obedience as the condition of the covenant?
- Why is death the only possible consequence of failure to give God perfect obedience?

What happened in the greatest disaster?

Did Adam obey God or not? If you have read Genesis 2 and 3 you will already know whether Adam kept the terms of the covenant God made with him. In this chapter we will continue to follow the story of Genesis as the Catechism deals with it in Question 13 and Question 15, before coming back to Question 14 in the next chapter.

13 Did our first parents continue in the estate wherein they were created?

Our first parents, being left to the freedom of their own will, fell from the estate wherein they were created, by sinning against God.

15 What was the sin whereby our first parents fell from the estate wherein they were created?

The sin whereby our first parents fell from the estate wherein they were created, was their eating the forbidden fruit.

Choice

Before Adam sinned he did not have a sinful nature or sinful desires. Adam and Eve were left to the *"freedom of their own will."* Adam's will had the freedom to choose

> "They could choose to obey God or disobey God."

whatever it wanted, unconstrained by anything other than his own nature. Although it was perfect, the possibility was left open that it could change. Adam and Eve had the freedom and the ability to choose between good and evil. They could choose to obey God or disobey God. They could heed what God had said about that one particular *"tree of the knowledge of good and evil"* or they could ignore His command not to eat of it. God left them to make this choice freely. He did not use any special power to direct them against their will, but He left them to choose as they wished.

Temptation

Satan was an angel who had sinned and been thrown out of heaven. Satan hated God and all that He had created. He appeared in the garden and through the serpent spoke to Eve. His aim was to cause Adam and Eve to sin. He could not force them to do wrong but he could tempt them to sin. That is exactly what he did. Satan bypassed Adam, the responsible leader, and approached Eve. He made the forbidden fruit seem very desirable to eat, and besides, he said that if they ate the fruit they would become wise (Genesis 3:5). He also flatly told her that it was not true that they would die if they ate the forbidden fruit (Genesis 3:4).

In this way Satan cunningly provided Adam and Eve with false and misleading stories which prompted them to change their minds about the goodness and trustworthiness of God. In the freedom of their own wills, they chose to sin against God by eating the forbidden fruit.

Fall

By eating the forbidden fruit, Adam and Eve sinned against God. This single act of disobedience included many other sins in it - horrible rebellion against their good and gracious creator, murder of themselves, covetousness and theft of what was not theirs to take, for example.

By sinning against God, Adam and Eve fell from the state in which they had been created. Adam and Eve's original state as created is sometimes called the state of innocence, because as we have seen, they were created perfect and holy. When we refer to *"The Fall,"* this is what is meant - the disastrous downward descent from a state of being holy and perfect at the peak of God's beautiful and pure creation, to a shameful state of sin and sorrow. Adam, and Eve fell from innocence to guilt, from perfection to being riddled with flaws, and from holiness to corruption.

> "By sinning against God, Adam and Eve fell from the state in which they had been created."

Change

For Adam and Eve life would never be the same again. They were once in a state of happy innocence but now they were in a state of sin and misery. In guilty fear they tried to hide from God. They knew they could no longer enjoy the favour and fellowship of their Maker as before. *"Adam and his wife hid themselves from the presence of the LORD God amongst the trees of the garden"* (Genesis 3:8). They were now slaves to sin and Satan, and were no longer able to obey God.

🔍 Something to think about...

- How was *'the freedom of their own will'* both a strength and a weakness for Adam and Eve?
- What makes Satan so dangerous?
- What was so bad about eating the forbidden fruit?

What is sin?

We have seen that Adam and Eve fell from their original state when they sinned against God. But what is sin anyway? Question 14 answers this from two perspectives.

> 💬 What is sin?
>
> Sin is any want of conformity unto, or transgression of, the law of God.

Benchmarks and boundaries

The *"law of God"* is all that God requires of us, which He has told us. We can think of it as various distinct commandments, or one unified law.

"God's law is something He has revealed. We don't have to guess at the contents of God's law."

Viewed in one way, God's law sets the benchmark we have to measure up to. We must *do* certain things. We have to conform to a particular standard or pattern. We have to meet a certain target.

Viewed in another way, God's law sets boundaries for us that we must not cross. We must *not* do certain things. We have to stay within the limits or parameters that He has specified.

God's law is something He has revealed. We don't have to guess at the contents of God's law. The whole Word of God is informative about what God requires from us, and it also gives precise lists (such as the Ten Commandments) which leave us in no doubt how we should live and behave.

Sin is doing what God forbids

Any *"transgression"* of the law of God is sin (1 John 3:4). If we drive through a red traffic light or ignore a sign that says, *'No trespassing,'* we are transgressing the law of the land. God's law sets boundaries for us that we must not transgress. We must not cross the boundary into idolatry, swearing, murder, lying, or covetousness. If we cross the boundary and do what God forbids, we are sinning.

"If we cross the boundary and do what God forbids we are sinning."

Sin is not doing what **God requires**

Any **"want"** (that is, lack) of conformity to the law of God is sin (James 4:17). When a darts player is aiming for the target, they won't be satisfied with hitting anything less than the bullseye. You might trace a line on some cloth before using scissors to cut it - if you veer away from the line, the amount you deviate is the amount you have spoiled the fabric. God's law is our benchmark. We have to love our neighbour, speak the truth, be content with what we have. When we fail to live up to this standard, our lack of conformity to God's law is our sin.

Many people never think of sin in this way. They think of sin only as transgressing the boundaries, not as swerving from the standard or deviating from the benchmark. Therefore they conclude that if they refrain from stealing or murdering they are not really sinners. They forget that falling short of what God requires is also sinful.

$\mathcal{Q}$ Something to think about...

- Write a quick list of several sins. Now identify whether each is a sin of *'lack of conformity'* or *'transgression'* in relation to God's law. Have you named more of one type than the other? (If so, can you balance the list by thinking of some others?)
- In Luke 10:30-32, Jesus told a parable about a man who journeyed from Jerusalem to Jericho. Think of how this man was treated by (a) the thieves, (b) the priest, and (c) the Levite. How did each of these show lack of conformity to God's law and/or transgression of it?
- The reference point for the Catechism's definition of sin is *'the law of God.'* Some people's reference point for sin is *'the harm it does to other people'* or *'the bad consequences it brings you.'* Why are these definitions inadequate? How did the good Samaritan show conformity to God's law?

Personal reflection
When you fail to do what God requires, do you think of this as real sin in the same way as when you do what God forbids?

Why is Adam's fall so important?

Adam and Eve made a terrible mistake in the Garden of Eden. But what relevance does this have for us? What connection do we have with Adam? Why is Adam's fall so important?

Did all mankind fall in Adam's first transgression?

The covenant being made with Adam, not only for himself, but for his posterity; all mankind, descending from him by ordinary generation, sinned in him, and fell with him, in his first transgression.

"Every one of Adam's posterity inherited a sinful nature."

Who are Adam's posterity?

Adam's posterity are all his descendants - his children, their children, all their children, and so on. The Bible tells us that God *"hath made of one blood all nations of men for to dwell on all the face of the earth"* (Acts 17:26). We have all come from Adam. If we go back far enough through our parents, grandparents, great-grandparents, great-great-grandparents, and so on, we will eventually arrive back after many generations to Adam and Eve as our first parents. This means that we are all part of the great family of the human race no matter where in the earth we live, or when in history we were born.

How was Adam our representative?

Adam was not only the ancestor and father of us all, but he was also our representative. When God made the covenant of life with him, Adam was not simply an individual solely responsible for himself, he was acting on behalf of all his posterity (his role is sometimes referred to as the 'covenant head' or the 'federal head' of all his descendants). Perhaps one or two illustrations will go some way to help us understand the principle of representation. When decisions need to be taken about how our country is run, each local area chooses somebody to represent them in parliament. We send our representatives to sit as Members of Parliament in London and Members of the Scottish Parliament in Edinburgh, for example. Our representatives speak, vote, and take decisions on our behalf. We do not sit in parliament ourselves; our representatives are there in our place.

Similarly, when our country takes part in the Olympics, expert coaches choose only the best and most competent sports people to represent us. When someone from Team GB wins a medal, their success is a source of honour and pride for the whole country. A single athlete winning gold gives the nation, as a whole, a sense of achievement, because of the way in which that athlete represents us.

Adam was the best and most competent representative we could have had. He was selected by God to act and take decisions on behalf of all of us. If he had succeeded in passing the test of obedience, all his posterity would have been included in the reward he earned as their representative. But since he failed on our behalf, his failure affects us all.

How did Adam's fall **affect his posterity?**

Because Adam was our representative, we are all affected by his actions. When he committed his transgression, all his posterity sinned in him and fell with him. Everyone he represented was included *"in him."* Whatever he did on our behalf, we did *'in him.'* When he sinned, we sinned in him. When he broke the covenant, we broke the covenant in him. His actions have consequences for all of us. We fell with him. He fell from holiness and innocence into sin and corruption, and we fell with him. We have inherited from Adam a sinful and corrupt nature. As Paul explains, *"by one man's disobedience many were made sinners"* (Romans 5:19), not because of some arbitrary connection, but because Adam was our covenant head.

Have there been any **exceptions?**

For several thousand years after Adam there were no exceptions. Every one of Adam's posterity inherited a sinful nature. *"For all have sinned, and come short of the glory of God"* (Romans 3:23). The disease of sin was transmitted from one generation to the next (Psalm 51:5). But eventually one was born who *"did no sin"* (1 Peter 2: 22). This was the Lord Jesus Christ.

All of those who are descended from Adam by ordinary generation, are included in Adam's sin and fall, without exception. But Jesus Christ did not descend from Adam by ordinary means i.e., as the child of a human father and a human mother. Although Jesus was a real human with an ordinary (sinful) human mother, He did not have a human father. Therefore Adam's sin was not transmitted to Him. The angel told Mary the mother of Jesus that, *"the Holy Ghost shall come upon thee, and the power of the Highest shall overshadow thee: therefore also that holy thing which shall be born of thee shall be called the Son of God"* (Luke 1:35).

> "All of those who are descended from Adam by ordinary generation, are included in Adam's sin and fall, without exception."

As we move on through the Catechism, we will discover that Jesus Christ is a real man, and yet a sinless man. This brings hope into this dreadfully bleak picture of the entirely lost, ruined and sinful state of the human race.

🔍 Something to think about...

- What dual relationship do we all have with Adam?
- Sometimes people resent the fact that Adam acted on their behalf and implicated them in his fall before they were even born. So imagine that instead, God had made a covenant of life with each human being individually. Would this arrangement actually put anyone in a better position than Adam to fulfil the covenant successfully?
- If Adam had not sinned, he would have been rewarded with life for himself and all his descendants. What legacy has he bequeathed to us instead?
- Who is the only man who has ever been born by *'extraordinary generation'* and what consequence does this have for his inheriting Adam's sinfulness and fallen nature?

Personal reflection

When you think of the dreadful effects of Adam's sin, are you more inclined (a) to resent Adam and his grossly irresponsible behaviour, or (b) to hate and dread sin? Which response is the more appropriate?

How does Adam's fall affect us?

In Questions 13-15 we looked at how Adam fell. In Question 16 we looked at who all has been affected by the fall. Now in Question 17 the Catechism begins to explore the consequences of the fall.

17 Into what estate did the fall bring mankind?

The fall brought mankind into an estate of sin and misery.

The fall brought **darkness**

Satan promised Adam and Eve something much better than they already had. He dangled before them the prospect of having their eyes opened - of better knowledge, better light. But instead they found themselves in a state of sin, where all they could do was sin, and sin more. The first thing they saw with their newly opened eyes was their shame. Their new knowledge of good and evil was not a positive thing. Their innocence was taken away, and all they wanted to do was hide, under cover, away from God and his holiness and goodness.

The fall brought **distress**

In the moment Adam and Eve sinned, all the happiness they had previously enjoyed in God and His creation evaporated. Sin always brings misery along with it. There would be no such thing as misery if there was no such thing as sin. God told Eve and Adam individually that they would each have a life of hardship and sorrow, and eventually their bodies would return to the dust they came from. Instead of leading an exciting new life *"as gods,"* as Satan promised, they doomed themselves to all sorts of distress, culminating in death.

> "Sin always brings misery along with it."

Q Something to think about...

- Sin breeds more sin, and is always accompanied by misery. Can you think of some examples of this, either from the Bible or everyday life?

Personal reflection

By nature we hate to be reminded of the consequences of the fall. These truths leave us troubled and uncomfortable. But we cannot escape from them and need to face up to the reality of sin and its consequences. Does your sense of discomfort and of the unpleasantness of sin make you hate sin? Does it make you long to be reconciled to God?

How sinful are we?

In the previous chapter we looked at the tragic results of the fall and saw that it brought us into a state of sin and misery. We now come to consider in more detail the "sin" aspect of this state of sin and misery. How can we analyse or classify the sinfulness of our fallen state? Question 18 tells us that our sinfulness includes two things - original sin and actual sin.

> **18** Wherein consists the sinfulness of that estate whereinto man fell?
>
> The sinfulness of that estate whereinto man fell, consists in the guilt of Adam's first sin, the want of original righteousness, and the corruption of his whole nature, which is commonly called Original Sin; together with all actual transgressions which proceed from it.

What is original sin?

Original sin has three aspects to it, according to Question 18.

1. Original sin includes **"the guilt of Adam's first sin."** If Adam had met the condition of the covenant, everyone he represented would have been credited with his righteousness. His righteousness would have been imputed to them, assigned to them, treated as if it belonged to them. But Adam sinned. So the guilt of Adam's sin is imputed to everyone he represented. The guilt of Adam's first sin belongs to all of us by imputation.

    It is however only the guilt of Adam's **"first sin"** which is imputed to us. Once Adam sinned, he ceased to represent us as our covenant head. So none of Adam's subsequent sins are imputed to his descendants. They were solely his own private responsibility.

2. Original sin includes the **"want (or lack) of original righteousness."**

"Whatever part of our nature you think of, in soul or body, we are defiled by sin."

Adam's original righteousness was his uprightness, purity, and perfect conformity to God. But Adam's descendants lack all of this. **"There is none righteous, no, not one"** (Romans 3:10). We lack spiritual discernment, we lack the inclination to do good, and we lack any love for holiness. This lack and these failures are classified as part of our sinfulness, partly because (as we have seen) any lack of conformity to God's law is sin, and partly because we lost this righteousness voluntarily.

3. Original sin includes **"the corruption of our whole nature."** It's not just that we lack holiness - we are actively and thoroughly corrupt. While our lack of original righteousness explains our lack of desire to do what is right, our

45

depravity is what explains our positive inclination to do wrong. Whatever part of our nature you think of, in soul or body, we are defiled by sin. This is why **'the corruption of his whole nature'** is sometimes called *'total depravity.'* It is not that we are always as totally wicked as we could possibly be, but we are depraved in the totality of our being. Imagine a glass filled with water. The water is pure and safe to drink. However if deadly poison is added to the water, it is no longer pure but polluted in its entirety.

Both our lack of original righteousness and our depravity belong to us, not by imputation, but inherently. Adam's guilt is imputed to us – it is added to our account, it is something that we are made responsible for because of our covenant relationship with him. But what we have inherently is ours personally; it resides in us, it is ingrained. This aspect of original sin — our lack of righteousness and total corruption — is not just written on our charge sheet, it's woven into the fabric of our hearts.

What is **actual sin?**

Our sinfulness includes not only original sin, but also *"all actual transgressions."* Actual transgressions are acts of sin. These acts include thoughts and words as well as deeds and behaviours, in both sins of omission (omitting a duty) and sins of commission (committing a transgression).

Actual sins *"proceed from"* original sin, as the Catechism says. As Jesus explained, **"Out of the heart proceed evil thoughts, murders, adulteries, fornications, thefts, false witness, blasphemies..."** (Matthew 15:19). Our corrupt nature is the source of all our sinful acts, in the same way as a polluted fountain sends out polluted streams, or a rotten tree produces rotten fruit.

How does *"actual sin"* differ from *"original sin?"* We have to realise that the word *'actual'* here does not mean *'real, factual,'* as if original sin was by contrast something vague or imaginary. Original sin is as entirely real as actual sins. But original sin refers to our disposition, while actual sin refers to our actions. Original sin is sometimes called *'the sin of our nature'* and actual sin is sometimes called *'the sin of our practice.'*

"Original sin is as entirely real as actual sins."

🔍 Something to think about...

- Is it fair that we are all held guilty because of Adam's first sin?
- Every part of our nature is defiled by sin. How do we observe this in: (a) how we think, (b) how we make decisions, (c) what we like and dislike?
- To solve the problem of our sinfulness, is it enough to simply deal with outward acts? What needs to be done in order to tackle the problem of our sin at its root?

Personal reflection

If our corrupt nature is the source of all our sinful acts, this must mean that our sinful acts are just 'the tip of the iceberg.' Do you give enough attention to what lurks beneath the surface of your heart, or would you be satisfied with yourself if your acts seemed generally respectable to other people?

How miserable are we?

Now that we have looked at the sinfulness of our fallen state in Question 18, we turn in Question 19 to look at the misery, sadness, and distress the fall has brought us into. The word 'misery' captures well the terrible, awful situation in which we find ourselves. We are indeed in a miserable state.

19 What is the misery of that estate whereinto man fell?

All mankind by their fall lost communion with God, are under his wrath and curse, and so made liable to all the miseries of this life, to death itself, and to the pains of hell for ever.

"Before Adam and Eve sinned, they enjoyed unspoiled friendship and communion with God."

The fellowship we have lost

Before Adam and Eve sinned, they enjoyed unspoiled friendship and communion with God. They were in total harmony with their Maker. But sin ended that harmony and they no longer enjoyed the company of God. The relationship between God and man was no longer what it had been. The bond of love and trust was broken. Human beings were now rebels with sinful hearts, lives and desires, and God no longer delighted in them.

Adam and Eve hid themselves amongst the trees of the garden after they had sinned (Genesis 3:8-10). As they cowered, trying to hide from God, they experienced the misery of lost communion and were afraid.

The wrath and curse we are under

The consequence of being under God's wrath is that we are under God's curse. God's curse is the punishment given out to those whom God is displeased with. The Bible tells us, **"Cursed is every one that continueth not in all things which are written in the book of the law to do them"** (Galatians 3:10). Being under a curse is the opposite of being under a blessing. In Deuteronomy 28, the blessings listed in verses 3-16 have precise counterpoints in the curses in verses 16-19. As the blessings that would have come on covenant-keepers are very wide-ranging, so the curses on covenant-breakers are similarly sweeping. Ours is not a straightforward path of fulfillment and contentment as we successfully achieve meaningful goals in our projects and relationships. We are instead blighted with difficulties, failure, frustration, and futility.

At home and in business, in matters physical and psychological, on both economic and societal fronts, in domestic and international affairs — in all our activities, and across every aspect of our existence — fallen humanity is under the wrath and curse of God.

The distresses we are exposed to

Sorrow

You just have to open a newspaper or watch the news to see some of the miseries of this life. In one place there may be drought and famine, and in another war and disasters. The history of the world is a story of lives ruined through violence, stealing, cheating, and immorality.

As individuals we are prone to health problems, difficulties with our finances and property, troubles and bereavement in our families. Spiritually, we suffer from blindness of mind, aversion to good, a love of sin, and hardness of heart. These are all examples of the sorrows we are *"liable to."* This means we are subject to them by law, or legally left 'wide open' to experiencing them. But they are just a few examples. We are, in fact, liable to *"all the miseries of this life,"* and all because of our sin.

Death

We are not only exposed to miseries in this life. At the end of our lives, we are exposed to death, which is itself a misery. Death is the separation of our souls from our bodies. This disrupts the unity of the human person and is therefore intrinsically a dreadful thing. But sin and death are inseparably connected. Ezekiel reminds us, *"The soul that sinneth, it shall die"* (18:4). Paul points out that death is simply *"the wages of sin"* (Romans 6:23). Our wages are what we have earned, or what we deserve.

Danger

A miserable life, and the misery of death - will the sorrow of our fallen state come to an end after that? No. The Catechism reminds us that because of our sin we are in danger of the pains of hell for ever. We are condemned as law-breakers by a holy God. There is no excuse and there will be no hiding place. The punishment of the broken law will continue on throughout the endless ages of eternity in the pains of hell. Hell is the place of endless punishment prepared by God for the devil and his angels, a place in which they will be joined by all those who share their rebellion against God. Hell is the blackness of darkness forever; a place to be avoided at all costs. No wonder it says in Hebrews 10:31 that *"It is a fearful thing to fall into the hands of the living God."* *"Where is hell?"* a sceptic once scornfully asked a Christian. He replied, At the end of a Christ-less life.

> "Where is hell? At the end of a Christ-less life."

🔍 Something to think about...

- Sin invariably brings misery. How should this help us to hate sin?
- Life is not, in fact, utter, unremitting misery. Considering what we are liable to as sinners, how should this help us to be thankful to God?
- Death is sad because it brings bereavement. But is this the worst thing about death?
- Why is it not disproportionate for sinners to have to undergo *"the pains of hell for ever"?*

Personal reflection
If you had to rank all the sad things in your life in order from most serious to least serious, where would you put loss of communion with God'? Why?

What is God's plan of salvation?

The fall brought us, quite justly, into a state of appalling sin and terrible misery. Questions 17 to 19 have made for very grim reading and sombre reflection. But is there any way of escape? Question 20 throws open the door of hope by telling us what God has done so that not all of mankind will perish in their sins.

20 Did God leave all mankind to perish in the estate of sin and misery?

God having, out of his mere good pleasure, from all eternity, elected some to everlasting life, did enter into a covenant of grace, to deliver them out of the estate of sin and misery, and to bring them into an estate of salvation by a Redeemer.

God's wonderful **mercy**

Did God leave the whole human race to perish in the state of sin and misery? No! God is so merciful that He chose not to condemn the whole human race to a lost eternity. It was not His will that all should perish. Rather He has *"elected some"* or chosen a certain number who would be saved, and would not receive what they deserved.

Why did God choose to do this? Simply because it pleased Him to do so. It was His *"mere good pleasure."* The Bible makes this clear: *"having predestinated us unto the adoption of children by Jesus Christ to himself, according to the good pleasure of his will"* (Ephesians 1: 5). Those saved by God did not deserve to be chosen any more than others. It is not because of anything good or special about them. It is not because they were more needy than others. It is not because He saw that they would be, or do anything, good after they were saved. The reason lies entirely in God Himself.

In the Word of God we discover that this choice, or election, has existed from all

> "Those saved by God did not deserve to be chosen any more than others."

eternity: *"He hath chosen us in him before the foundation of the world"* (Ephesians 1:4). It was always so, even before each individual was born, and before the world was. As the Lord said to Jeremiah, *"I have loved thee with an everlasting love"* (Jeremiah 31:3).

God's wonderful **plan**

God entered *"a covenant of grace."* The first covenant in human history was the covenant God made with Adam. But after Adam broke that covenant, a new revelation was made of another covenant - *"the covenant of grace."* This covenant, although it was announced second, was actually made first. It was made in eternity, according to God's *"mere good pleasure."*

As we saw in Question 12, the covenant made with Adam was variously called the covenant of life (because it promised life), or the covenant of works (because it required works from Adam). This one is called the covenant of grace, because it originates in the free grace of God and it gives salvation to sinners on the basis of free grace.

Just like we did with the covenant of works, we can identify the different ingredients of the covenant of grace. In the covenant of grace, the persons making the agreement are God the Father and Jesus Christ, God the Son. The condition was that Christ would provide the perfect obedience demanded in the first covenant and pay the penalty of the broken first covenant. The consequences if Christ met the condition would be glory for Christ and life for his people, otherwise disgrace and death.

In both covenants, our participation in the consequences depends entirely on our connection with the representative and whether he succeeds in meeting the condition of the covenant. In the first covenant, Adam represented all his posterity. In the second covenant, Christ represents all his spiritual children, those who are elected to everlasting life.

God's wonderful news

The good news of the gospel is that we can be saved from our state of sin and misery. We can be brought out of that state and into the state of salvation. God can deal with our sinfulness – our guilt can be removed, our corrupt nature can be changed, Our actual transgressions continue in this life, although we abhor them; they will only stop in the life to come, if we are saved. God can deal with our misery – communion with Himself can be restored, His wrath can be turned away and His curse turned into blessing, and we can enjoy happiness in this life, at death, and in the life to come.

All this is achieved *"by a Redeemer."* The work of a redeemer is a combination of buying something back from slavery (by paying the price) and rescuing someone from captivity (by a powerful conquest). As we will see in the next chapter, the Redeemer of God's people is the Lord Jesus Christ. No one who comes to Christ for salvation will be turned away. *"For God so loved the world, that he gave his only begotten Son, that whosoever believeth in him should not perish, but have everlasting life"* (John 3:16).

> "The good news of the gospel is that we can be saved from our state of sin and misery."

The Catechism will now take several questions to look in more detail at who the Redeemer is and how He redeems His people (Questions 21-28), before turning to focus on how we are made partakers of this redemption (Questions 29-38).

🔍 Something to think about...

- Why is *'the covenant of grace'* an appropriate name for God's arrangement to save sinners?
- Draw two columns, one headed *'covenant of works'* and the other headed *'covenant of grace.'* Now fill in the following pieces of information for each covenant, referring back to Question 12 if you need to.

    (a) Who are the persons making the agreement?
    (b) What is the condition?
    (c) What are the consequences of successfully fulfilling the condition?
    (d) What are the consequences of failure to meet the condition?
    (e) Who is represented by the persons making the agreement?

Personal reflection

Does the thought of your state of sin and misery make you long to be firmly delivered into the state of salvation?

Are you thankful for God's mere good pleasure which chooses to deliver some sinners from perishing? Do you admire the amazing love of the triune God for self-destroying sinners?

Who is the only Redeemer?

Question 20 made the announcement that God saves sinners by a Redeemer. Now in Question 21 we come to focus more closely on who this Redeemer is.

> **21** Who is the Redeemer of God's elect?
>
> The only Redeemer of God's elect is the Lord Jesus Christ, who, being the eternal Son of God, became man, and so was, and continueth to be, God and man in two distinct natures, and one person, for ever.

"No one who was only human could do what the covenant of grace required — provide a perfect righteousness and bear the weight of the penalty of the broken law."

There is **a Redeemer**

Because of the broken covenant of works, we find ourselves menaced by a great number of fierce enemies who keep us enslaved and in captivity. We need to be redeemed from our iniquities (Psalm 130:8), from the curse of the law (Galatians 3:13), from destruction (Psalm 103:4), and from the power of the grave and death (Hosea 13:14).

Christ is described here as the Redeemer. This description takes us to the very heart of His work as the Saviour of sinners. To redeem us, He has to both pay a ransom and win a victory. The price He pays is the sacrifice of Himself (1 Peter 1:18-19). The victory He wins is a triumphant rescue of captives from mighty warriors and terrible tyrants (Isaiah 49:25-26). Both perfectly qualified and completely victorious, He has **"by his own blood ... obtained eternal redemption for us"** (Hebrews 9:12).

Here the Redeemer is named as the Lord Jesus Christ. He is the Lord Jehovah. He is Jesus, the man who was born to save His people from their sins. He is the Christ, the Messiah, the One whom God commissioned to be mediator and Saviour.

He is **the eternal Son of God**

Christ is the eternal Son of God. From all eternity, he has always been the Son of God, the second person of the Trinity. He never became the Son of God - not when He became man, nor at any point in His existence, nor at any time in the history of the universe. As the eternal Son, He is God, in the same way as the Father is God and the Spirit is God. As the eternal Son, He is not and never has been subordinate to the Father in any way.

He became **man**

To do the work of redemption, *"the eternal Son of God became man."* He became a real man. He did not just look like a man — He really was a man. *"The Word was made flesh"* (John 1:14). He was born in Bethlehem and lived an ordinary human life: growing up from childhood to adulthood, eating and drinking, working, becoming tired, resting, holding conversations with friends, and keeping up relationships within his family.

It was necessary for the Redeemer to be a man. For one thing, if He was going to be able to act as the representative of human beings, He needed to be a member of the human race, moreover, He needed to be able to do things that God cannot do — obey the law, suffer, and die.

But it was impossible for the Redeemer to be a mere man, or only human. It was also necessary for the Redeemer to be God. For one thing, no one who was only human could do what the covenant of grace required — provide a perfect righteousness and bear the weight of the penalty of the broken law. Furthermore, the value of His work would not have been sufficient for the needs of all the people He was representing in the covenant, if He was not God.

He is God and man **in one person**

The eternal Son of God is a *divine person* - the second person of the Trinity. This divine person took on a *human nature*. It is important to understand that he did not become a *human person* - he remained the same divine person he had always been, i.e., God the Son. Human nature is what all humans have in common (in particular a body and a soul). The eternal Son of God took a human nature into union with his divine person. This means that our Saviour is a divine person, not a human person. It means also that our Saviour is *one person* (with two natures), not two persons.

Christ has two natures, both a divine nature and a human nature. The two natures are not converted into each other, or compounded into a hybrid, or mixed together. His divine nature remains truly and fully divine, while His human nature is truly and fully human. Christ is really God and really man. Yet he is one person, Christ.

Not only was it necessary for the Redeemer to be God, and necessary for the Redeemer to be man, but it is necessary for the Redeemer to be God and man in one person. This is because His work was to reconcile God and man. It is also so that God can accept the works He did according to each nature (e.g., the value of his divinity, or the obedience of his humanity) as done on behalf of humans. It is also so that we can rely on these works as the works of one whole person, Christ.

Although this union of two natures in one person had a beginning in time (at the time of the incarnation), it is a union which will last for ever. Our Redeemer was God as well as man when He lived on this earth. Our Redeemer is man as well as God in heaven now. And our Redeemer will continue to be the God-man forever.

> "There is only one Saviour and only one way to God, and all who reject this mediator are on the broad way which leads to destruction."

He is **the only Redeemer**

Christ is not just *a* Redeemer, He is the *only* Redeemer. *"For there is one God, and one mediator between God and men, the man Christ Jesus"* (1 Timothy 2:5). Nobody else was capable of achieving the work of redemption. Nobody else was authorised by God to take on the work of redemption. Christ, and He alone, was qualified, equipped, and commissioned to be Redeemer, and Christ himself successfully achieved redemption for His people. There is only one Saviour and only one way to God, and all who reject this mediator are on the broad way which leads to destruction. It is very common to hear people say that all religions lead to God. They think that as long as you follow your own preferred religious path sincerely, all will be well. That is not the message of God's Word. Acts 4:12 says, *"Neither is there salvation in any other: for there is none other name under heaven given among men, whereby we must be saved."*

Q Something to think about...

- People sometimes feel they are oppressed and held back by, e.g., their circumstances in life, bad experiences, other people's prejudices, or their own negative thought patterns. Can we expect to be redeemed from these things? What things does Christ primarily redeem His people from?
- Think of the eternal Son of God becoming man. What does this tell us about the grace of Christ? What does it tell us about the importance He attached to His people?
- Why did the Redeemer need to be God? Why did the Redeemer need to be man? Why did the Redeemer need to be God and man in one person?

Personal reflection
Christ is the only Redeemer there is. Does this make you want to have Him for yourself?

How did the Son of God become man?

It is a wonderful truth that the eternal Son of God became man. The eternal became limited by time. The infinite became constrained by space. The unchangeable experienced variation. The Almighty became a helpless infant. It amazed the angels as they worshipped Him at Bethlehem. It amazes us as we contemplate it. And even more so when we think that He did this voluntarily, because He wanted to redeem His people. This event is often referred to as the incarnation, when God was embodied in flesh.

💬 How did Christ, being the Son of God, become man?

Christ, the Son of God, became man, by taking to himself a true body, and a reasonable soul, being conceived by the power of the Holy Ghost, in the womb of the Virgin Mary, and born of her, yet without sin.

A real man

We saw in Question 21 that Christ took human nature. But what is human nature? It is what all humans have in common, a body and a soul. Our personality is what distinguishes each human being from the rest, whereas our nature is what all humans share in exactly the same way. Christ, already existing as a person in His own right, took a human body and soul into union with Himself.

Viewed from one perspective, this was a human nature which the Father had prepared for Him and which the Spirit formed in the womb of Mary. This is often referred to as the incarnation which means taking on flesh. From this perspective, all three persons of the Trinity were involved in creating the humanity of the Redeemer. But from a different perspective, Christ Himself took this human nature. It was His own personal act when He took this humanity into His divine person and united it to Himself.

He took to himself **a true body**

Christ's body was a real body of flesh, blood and bone. He did not simply have the appearance of a man, He had a real, physical body, just like anyone else's. He was born as a little baby and was a helpless infant who, in process of time, grew up. Like everyone else He was hungry at times, and ate and drank. Like everyone else He was tired and felt pain at times, and He had to rest and sleep.

> "Christ's body was a real body of flesh, blood and bone."

He took to himself a reasonable soul

As well as a true body, Christ took a true soul. The human soul is *"reasonable,"* i.e., rational, able to think, reason and understand. The human soul is also emotional, able to love, rejoice, grieve, etc. The human soul also includes the will, or the ability to choose and decide, and the conscience, or the ability to judge between right and wrong. When Christ took to Himself *"a reasonable soul,"* this means He had a human mind, human emotions, a human will, and a human conscience.

It was not that He had a human body and then His spiritual part was all His divine nature, as if the fact that He was God replaced the need for Him to have a soul. Isaiah spoke about His soul (Isaiah 53:12) and Christ spoke about His own soul in Matthew 26:38. When He became man, He became fully man, with a real body and a real soul.

A unique man

The Lord Jesus Christ became a real man but at the same time He was a unique man. Unlike everyone else, Christ was not conceived *"by ordinary generation"* (as we saw in Question 16). Everyone else is conceived in the ordinary biological process where a human father and a human mother produce a human child. But Christ had no human father. His human nature was miraculously conceived in Mary's womb by the power of the Holy Spirit. Of course, the Holy Spirit had no human nature that could contribute anything to the humanity of Christ, He is not the father of Christ's humanity. Although it is necessarily impossible for us to understand the details of what happened, we know as much as the angel told Mary, *"The Holy Ghost shall come upon thee, and the power of the Highest shall overshadow thee: therefore also that holy thing which shall be born of thee shall be called the Son of God"* (Luke 1:35).

The fact that Christ had a human mother meant that He really belongs to the human race. But the fact that His mother was a virgin meant that He was not affected by original sin.

A holy man

Christ was a real man, yet He was *"without sin"* (Hebrews 4:15). When the angel spoke to Mary he referred to Christ as *"holy."* He was entirely free from both original sin and actual sins. It can be hard for us to dissociate the concept of sinfulness from our understanding of humanity, since all around us is evidence of human sin. But sin is an intruder, it is not something that belongs to human nature as such. Christ, a real man, with real human nature, was a sinless man. He lived a holy life, committing no sin whatsoever.

No one was ever able to accuse Him of any sin. He never did a sinful thing, He never said a sinful word and He never had a sinful thought. He lived in a sinful world but was never in any way contaminated by it.

> "Christ, a real man, with real human nature, was a sinless man. He lived a holy life, committing no sin whatsoever."

Q Something to think about...

- The story of how Jesus was born can become so familiar that we fail to see the wonder of it. Why should we be amazed at the incarnation?
- How does the fact that Christ is a real man help us to see Him as someone very close and very approachable?

Personal reflection
Does the sinlessness of Christ make you love Him? Does the sinlessness of Christ encourage you to be holy yourself?

How is Christ a prophet?

Having been taught that a Redeemer has been provided for sinners, we are shown in the next section of the Catechism how the Redeemer saves His people (Questions 23-28). In Question 24 we see especially how Christ teaches us what we need to know for salvation.

23 What offices doth Christ execute as our Redeemer?

Christ, as our Redeemer, executeth the offices of a prophet, of a priest, and of a king, both in his estate of humiliation and exaltation.

24 How doth Christ execute the office of a prophet?

Christ executeth the office of a prophet, in revealing to us, by his Word and Spirit, the will of God for our salvation.

Three offices in two estates

Question 23 tells us that Christ executes certain offices. Here, **"offices"** means roles or functions. To **"execute"** them means to perform, or carry out, or do the work involved in these roles. As our Redeemer, Christ performs the functions of a prophet, of a priest, and of a king. These functions are the answer to our triple problem of ignorance, guilt, and captivity. We will look at each of the three offices in turn in Questions 24, 25, and 26.

Question 23 also tells us that Christ carries out His work **"both in his estate of humiliation and exaltation."** His **"humiliation"** refers to His time on earth when He humbled Himself. His **"exaltation"** refers to His state now that He is in heaven after successfully finishing the work of redemption. So Christ was a prophet, priest, and king when He was on earth, and He is a prophet, a priest, and a king in heaven now. We will look in more detail at these states in Questions 27 and 28.

Christ teaches us the will of God for our salvation

A prophet is God's mouthpiece - someone who takes a message from God to deliver to human beings. The prophets in the Old Testament often delivered a message which foretold future events. Often too they brought messages of rebuke. But the revelations God gave through the prophets include other elements too - words of encouragement and explanation of the people's current situation, for example. The basic job of a prophet is to reveal the will of God, whatever that will includes.

When Christ takes on the role of prophet, **"in revealing to us, by his Word and Spirit, the will of God for our salvation."** He teaches us everything that God wishes us to know, believe and do in order to be saved.

Christ's work as a prophet tackles our sinful ignorance. We need things to be revealed for our salvation because we don't know them otherwise and our blinded minds make us incapable of receiving them.

Christ teaches us **by His Word**

How does Christ teach us **"the will of God for our salvation"**? By His Word and Spirit. Christ's Word is the Bible. We are used to calling the Bible **"the Word of God,"** but it is also **"the Word of Christ."** It was given by Christ's Spirit and Christ is its core subject matter.

> "When we hear the Word of Christ opened up to us ... we should receive it in such a way that it can have its intended effect, our salvation."

The Bible is a complete revelation of what God wants us to know for salvation. It teaches us how we came to be sinners, it tells us what kind of sinners we are, and it warns us of the eternal consequences of sin. It also teaches us the way of salvation - who saves us, how He saves us, how we come into possession of salvation for ourselves, and the implications of being saved in this life and eternity. There is nothing we need to know for salvation which is not included in the Bible.

The Bible is also the only revelation of God's will for our salvation. Christ has not given us multiple revelations in different sources. We need no other book, teacher, or prophet, whether that be the Qur'an, the Book of Mormon, or the Pope. These sources are not the Word of Christ.

How do we access Christ's revelation in His Word? By reading it and by hearing it preached. When we read the Bible or hear it preached faithfully, Christ is speaking to us. This means that as readers, we should approach the Word reverently and respectfully and with the expectation that Christ will use His Word to reveal to us personally what God wants us to know for our salvation. It also means that preachers are not to come to the pulpit with their own ideas; they are to take great care to preach only the Word that God has given. To be faithful to Christ's purpose in giving His Word, preachers should focus on preaching things that are important for salvation - whether for the conversion of unbelievers or the building up of believers. As hearers we are to give heed only to what agrees with the Bible. In the Book of Acts (17:11) we read of the Jews at Berea who on hearing Paul preach made sure that what they were hearing was according to the Word of God. When we hear the Word of Christ opened up to us by one of Christ's preachers, we should receive it in such a way that it can have its intended effect — our salvation.

Christ teaches us **by His Spirit**

But why do so many people read the Word and hear it preached, yet still remain unbelievers? This is because Christ does not carry out His prophetic work by the Word alone. The Word is like a light shining brightly in a room full of blind people. As bright as it shines, it cannot give eyesight to the blind. So Christ as our prophet also works by His Spirit. The Holy Spirit takes away our sinful blindness. He gives us spiritual eyesight to see the truth in all its beauty and trustworthiness.

The Spirit does not normally save people apart from the Word (1 Peter 1:23-25). Although this is possible in extraordinary cases (for example when people are unable to understand the Word because of cognitive impairments or because they are infants), the general rule is that the Spirit uses the Word to save. Ordinarily we cannot expect the Spirit to bless anyone in the absence of the Word or in a way that contradicts the Word.

Christ therefore uses both His Word to give us the information we need and His Spirit to give us the understanding we need, to put us in possession of the will of God for our salvation. *"The natural man receiveth not the things of the Spirit of God: for they are foolishness unto him"* (1 Corinthians 2:14). But when Christ works by His Word and Spirit, we willingly receive the revelation of God's will for our salvation.

"The Word is like a light shining brightly in a room full of blind people. As bright as it shines, it cannot give eyesight to the blind."

Q Something to think about...

*   'The Word of Christ, without His Spirit, cannot teach us the will of God for our salvation; the Spirit of Christ, without His Word, will not.' Can you explain?

Personal reflection
"If any of you lack wisdom, let him ask of God, that giveth to all men liberally, and upbraideth not; and it shall be given him." (James 1:5). When we see that Christ is full of wisdom and full of patience, why would we hesitate to ask Him to teach us the will of God for our salvation?

Christ is our priest

The Lord Jesus Christ as the Redeemer of His people carries out three offices. Having looked at Christ in his prophetic office we now consider Christ as priest. The Catechism identifies the two parts of a priest's work: offering a sacrifice and making intercession.

25 How doth Christ execute the office of a priest?

Christ executeth the office of a priest, in his once offering up of himself a sacrifice to satisfy divine justice, and reconcile us to God; and in making continual intercession for us.

Christ offered a sacrifice

A priest

The work of a priest is to deal with God on behalf of the guilty. This means that a priest differs from a prophet in two ways: **(1)** A prophet represents God to man, while a priest represents man to God; and **(2)** while we need a prophet because of our ignorance, we need a priest because of our guilt.

A sacrifice

A priest has to do two things - offer a sacrifice, and make intercession. Question 25 tells us that when Christ carried out the role of a priest, the sacrifice He offered up was Himself. *"He offered up himself"* (Hebrews 7:27). He Himself was both the priest and the sacrifice. He offered Himself, the *"himself"* who is the God-man, two distinct natures in one person. When we think of the sacrifice as involving suffering and death, we are thinking of His human nature. When we think of the sacrifice as having infinite dignity and merit, we are thinking of His divine nature. So although only His humanity suffered and died, it did so as personally united to His divinity.

A satisfaction

One of the two intended effects of Christ's sacrifice was *"to satisfy divine justice."* God in His justice always requires perfect obedience to the law. Given the broken covenant of works, God in His justice additionally required someone to pay the penalty of death which is due to disobedience.

Christ as our priest provided both these things on our behalf - both obedience and death. He honoured God's law by keeping it constantly (every moment of His time on earth) and completely (in every nuance of every commandment, with all His mind, soul, heart, and strength, and in thought, word, and deed). He paid the penalty due to the broken covenant of works when His blood was shed and He died the cursed death of the cross — thus divine justice was satisfied.

A reconciliation

The other intended effect of Christ's sacrifice was to *"reconcile us to God."* The holy God is rightly angry with sinners, and sinners are hostile to the holy God (for no good reason, but just because of our sinfulness). When Christ satisfied God's justice, the consequence is that sinners are reconciled to God. God and sinners are made friends again. They are brought back together, peace is restored, the quarrel is settled, the differences are removed.

A final sacrifice

Christ made this sacrifice of Himself once. In the Old Testament system of sacrifices, there were many in-built limitations in both the priests and the sacrifices. They provided only a small scale model of how Christ and His sacrifice were going to work, demonstrating how ceremonial guilt could be ceremonially removed by animal sacrifices. These sacrifices had to be repeated often, because they were simply demonstrations, and could never be sufficient to actually remove the guilt of sin. But there were no limitations in either the priesthood or the sacrifice of Christ. In contrast to the Old Testament priests, who came daily, *"offering oftentimes the same sacrifices, which can never take away sins," Christ "offered one sacrifice for sins for ever"* (Hebrews 10:11-12). When He offered Himself that one time, He perfectly satisfied the justice of God for ever.

Christ intercedes

Ongoing

After the sacrifice is offered, the priest's work is not complete. It also includes *"making intercession."* Christ interceding for His people means He is speaking to God on their behalf, so as to bring them the benefits He wishes them to have, on the basis of His sacrifice.

Christ as our priest makes *"continual intercession for us."* This is His ongoing work. He has gone *"into heaven itself, now to appear in the presence of God for us"* (Hebrews 9:24). He hasn't forgotten His people now that He is in heaven. He is ceaselessly active on their behalf. They are never out of His thoughts for a moment. He is constantly advocating for them, standing up for them, and speaking up for them.

On the basis of the sacrifice

We get a glimpse of the way that Christ our intercessor speaks from His prayer in John 17. He says, *"Father, I will that they ... be with me where I am"* (John 17:24). This shows us not only that He wants the best possible blessings for His people (that they would be with Him and see His glory), but also that He asks authoritatively. He does not have to implore or cajole, but He simply expresses His will.

But why should the Father listen when Christ asks for a blessing for His sinful people? Because Christ has satisfied divine justice. He intercedes on the basis of His sacrifice of Himself which satisfied divine justice. *"We have an advocate with the Father, Jesus Christ the righteous: and he is the propitiation for our sins"* (1 John 2:1-2). It's not that He has to find some extenuating factors to make His people seem less sinful than they are. Nor does He try to talk up their human frailties so that they can get more lenient treatment than they deserve. Instead He points to His sacrifice and asks the Father to bless them for His sake. His satisfaction is so complete, and so full of merit, that when He appears in God's presence with His blood and the other evidences of His obedience and death, He only needs to say, *"I will..."* and the blessing He is interceding for is rightfully given.

The merit of Christ's sacrifice is also what guarantees the success of His intercession. He asks for nothing which He has not already fully paid the price for. What He asks for, He has earned - His people's complete salvation. We never need to worry that one of Christ's requests will be turned down.

On our behalf

Christ makes continual intercession *"for us."* This means everyone whom He is representing as Redeemer. They are innumerably many, and they have endless, complicated needs. But He does not get impatient with their little worries and He does not get worn out by their weighty problems. His intercession is skilful, holy, compassionate, and delivers at the right time. Because of Christ's intercession, sinners are saved in the first place, and then they receive daily pardon of sin, protection from Satan, growth in grace, peace and fellowship with God, God's approval of their service, and eventually complete and eternal salvation.

> "When He offered Himself that one time, He perfectly satisfied the justice of God for ever."

🔍 Something to think about...

- Divine justice would not have demanded Christ to suffer and die if it hadn't been for the fact that Christ had agreed to act as the Redeemer for His people. But what prompted Him to agree to this was grace, not justice. How should this help us to value Him in His work as a priest?
- Between God and the sinner there is a state of hostility. Why do we need both the obedience and the death of Christ in order to be reconciled to God?
- When we pray, we ask God to bless us *'for Christ's sake.'* When Christ intercedes for us, on the basis of His sacrifice, He is effectively asking *'for My sake.'* What is the connection between our prayers and Christ's intercession, and what encouragement can we take from this when we pray?

Personal reflection

Christ's work as a priest tackles our guilt. Have you ever realised that you are guilty in a way that led you to trust in Christ to be your priest?

Christ is **our king**

Jesus Christ, as the Redeemer of His people fulfils three offices. He does the work of a prophet, priest and king. Having looked at Christ in His prophetic and priestly roles we come now to consider Christ as a king.

The Bible frequently speaks of Christ as a king with a kingdom. We see this teaching in Old Testament passages such as Psalm 72 and Isaiah 9. Again in the New Testament the Lord speaks of His kingdom. He makes clear that His kingdom is not one that belongs to this world but is a spiritual kingdom (John 18:36). When the thief on the cross cried to the Lord, "Remember me when thou comest into thy kingdom" (Luke 23:42), Christ does not rebuke or correct him but speaking with all the authority of a king, assured him that his prayer would be answered.

In Question 26 we are told of three activities Christ performs as a king.

> **26** How doth Christ execute the office of a king?
>
> Christ executeth the office of a king, in subduing us to himself, in ruling and defending us, and in restraining and conquering all his and our enemies.

"They see how glorious and beautiful He is, and they willingly sign up on His side, giving Him their allegiance for ever."

Christ brings **His people into His kingdom**

If we need a prophet because of our ignorance and a priest because of our guilt, the reason we need a king is because of our rebelliousness. None of us are in Christ's kingdom until He brings us in.

As sinners we are in rebellion against the Lord. We are neither able nor willing to be the subjects of Christ. Paul explains that this is because, ***"the carnal mind is enmity against God: for it is not subject to the law of God, neither indeed can be"*** (Romans 8:7).

We have seen that as a priest, Christ makes reconciliation for His people by removing the reasons for estrangement between them and God. As a king, He removes the antagonism in their hearts against God. He destroys their natural hostility and makes them willing to receive Him and obey Him as their Lord and king.

Imagine someone applying for citizenship to a new country. They make all the arrangements to meet all the legal requirements. But they can still get their passport even while their heart is in their original country and they still feel foreign in the new country. It is different with Christ's kingdom. Not only does He meet all the legal requirements on a sinner's behalf, but He also gives them a new heart, so that they feel at home in His kingdom. He gives them a new birth, so that they are born a second time, born again into His kingdom. They are no more strangers and foreigners from grace, but their sense of identity and belonging is connected to Christ's kingdom and they are delighted to give their loyalty to Christ as their king.

How does Christ subdue sinners to Himself? On the one hand He comes in His power to release them from their spiritual predators and oppressors. These include the justice of God, the curse of the broken law, the tyranny of Satan, and their own sinfulness. Some of these enemies are simply cruel and unjust, but others rightly and lawfully hold sinners captive. Isaiah wonders, *"Shall the prey be taken from the mighty, and the lawful captive delivered?"* The answer from the Redeemer is a resounding, Yes! *"Even the captives of the mighty shall be taken away, and the prey of the terrible shall be delivered: for I will contend with him that contendeth with thee, and I will save thy children"* (Isaiah 49:24-26).

On the other hand, at the same time as He throws open the prison doors, He also wins their hearts. This too is a triumphant work of royal power. *"Thy people shall be willing in a day of thy power"* (Psalm 110:3). They see how glorious and beautiful He is, and they willingly sign up on His side, giving Him their allegiance for ever.

Christ rules and defends His people

Every king has laws for their subjects and Christ is no exception. For the guidance and safety of His own people He has given us the Bible as a rule of life. He says to His subjects, *"If ye love me, keep my commandments"* (John 14:15). By His Spirit working in their hearts, converts are able to love and obey their King more and more. They love Him as the One who has shown such great mercy in bringing them into His kingdom.

Christ also rules His people collectively. His kingdom does not consist of so many isolated individuals, but a community, the church. This is an organised community. Christ gives His church boundaries for membership, a system of government, and access to privileges ministers and elders who serve Him by teaching and disciplining His people. Christ is the only king and head of the church. No pope or monarch is the head of the church; and neither are church members free to do as they like. Christ is the One who lays out the rules for the church.

Christ also defends His people. He keeps them safe. *"The LORD is our defence"* (Psalm 89:18). Inside Christ's kingdom and under Christ's protection, absolutely nothing can destroy us, or do us any lasting damage. We can rely on His truth. We can refer everything to His justice. We can rest in His love. We can be sure of His omnipotence. In short, He Himself is our defence. *"For I, saith the LORD, will be unto her a wall of fire round about, and will be the glory in the midst of her"* (Zechariah 2:5).

Christ overcomes His people's enemies

Christ not only looks after His people inside His kingdom, He also wages war on all who are at enmity with Him and His people and defeats them. Their enemies include Satan, the world, death and the grave. They also include their own sin and self-destructiveness.

In fact, their enemies are His enemies. Christ and His people make up one body, so that anyone who tries to harm one of His people is essentially attacking Him, and those who hate Christ will correspondingly hate Christ's people.

Christ is well able to restrain all these enemies. He puts limits on them and holds them back from unleashing all the evil they desire to inflict on Him and His people. He is the all-powerful one, who is able to frustrate every plot and plan of His enemies.

Ultimately, Christ will not only restrain but completely conquer all His people's enemies. In one sense He has already conquered them. By His victorious death on the cross He *"spoiled principalities and powers, he made a show of them openly, triumphing over them in it"* (Colossians 2:15). Because of His victory, His people are already *"more than conquerors"* (Romans 8:37). But these enemies are still active and angry. We are still waiting for Christ to finish them off completely. They are like guerrillas and terrorists who keep up malicious sniper fire even after the war has been won. It is just a matter of time until they too are neutralised. Christ will eventually exterminate all the enemies of holiness and grace. All His enemies will be put under His feet (1 Corinthians 15:25). He does this with spiritual not physical

"He is the all-powerful one, who is able to frustrate every plot and plan of His enemies."

weapons, even sometimes making His enemies His friends by converting them. Confidently and thankfully we can say to Him, *"Thy kingdom is an everlasting kingdom, and thy dominion endureth throughout all generations"* (Psalm 145:13)

Q Something to think about...

- Christ brings people into His kingdom by release (from their enemies) and regeneration (i.e., the new birth). How do both these activities showcase His kingly skills?
- What makes Christ's people completely safe?
- Why is it dangerous to fight against Christ and Christ's people?

Personal reflection

Where do you belong? What community are you part of, and who are your people? Do you look at Christ's people and say what Ruth said to Naomi, *"Thy people shall be my people, and thy God my God"* (Ruth 1.16)?

How did Christ humble Himself?

As we saw in Question 23, Christ carries out the roles of prophet, priest and king in two states - the state of humiliation and the state of exaltation. Questions 27 and 28 look in more detail at each of these states.

---

27 Wherein did Christ's humiliation consist?

Christ's humiliation consisted in his being born, and that in a low condition, made under the law, undergoing the miseries of this life, the wrath of God, and the cursed death of the cross; in being buried, and continuing under the power of death for a time.

How did Christ humble Himself?

Jesus humbled Himself by coming down from the highest possible position to the lowest possible. The eternal Son of God, who is equal with the Father, humbled Himself when He became our Redeemer. His estate of humiliation is His 'humbleness,' or 'lowness,' the low position He took when He **"made himself of no reputation, and took upon him the form of a servant"** (Philippians 2:7). This is often referred to as a *'condescension,'* or a stooping down, or lowering of Himself. Question 27 lists several different ways that Christ humbled Himself.

> "The eternal Son of God ... humbled Himself when He became our Redeemer."

In His conception and birth

Christ is the eternal Son of God, yet He became man. He was born a helpless infant, dependent on Mary and Joseph to feed, clothe and care for Him. Let us pause for a moment and contemplate this astounding truth. Not only was Christ born, but also He was born **"in a low condition."** He was not born to a princess in a palace but to a poor woman in a stable. Many people are born into a state of poverty. There is nothing they can do about that. But in the case of Christ there is an important difference. He chose to be born in this low condition despite coming from the highest heaven (see Philippians 2:7-8).

In His life

Christ humbled Himself in His life by being **"made under the law."** As God, He was not under the law but the giver of the law. It was amazing condescension for the lawgiver to become subject to His own law, especially considering that He did so in order to obey it on behalf of those who had sinned against it.

It was also humbling for Christ to undergo **"the miseries of this life."** He did not lead a comfortable, indulgent life, but He lowered Himself to experience hunger and thirst, tiredness, pain, grief, and fear. He was tempted by Satan, who insulted both His identity and His work.

From wicked people He endured taunts, smear campaigns and abuse. This was so offensive to His holiness and so different to the peace and reverence He had left behind in heaven. His own relatives and His disciples misunderstood Him, and failed to recognise Him for who He was. He was then betrayed by a close confidant, someone who had claimed to be a friend, but who valued the worth of the Lord of glory at some thirty pieces of silver.

In His death

Christ humbled Himself by undergoing *"the wrath of God."* The wrath of God was a burden He carried throughout His life, but He felt it especially when it came to His death. On the cross, He was forsaken by His Father. This was an amazing humiliation for Christ, who had previously only known His Father's love.

Christ humbled Himself also by undergoing *"the cursed death of the cross."* It was a humiliation for the Lord of life to *die*. It was a humiliation for this glorious person to die *by crucifixion*, which was a notoriously shameful death. It was a humiliation for the blessed, beloved Lord to die under God's *curse.*

After death

Christ's state of humiliation did not end at death. After His death He was *"buried."* He was laid in the earth that He Himself had created. He lay in the grave, *"under the power of death,"* for three days. This was a humiliation because it appeared during those days as if He had failed, and had been conquered by death; because death would have had no power over Him at all, if it had not been for the sins of His people.

How did Christ work when He humbled Himself?

As we saw in Question 23, Christ carried out His roles of prophet, priest, and king in His state of humiliation.

He continued to act in each of these roles even though they were obscured and even sometimes openly ridiculed while He was here on earth.

Prophet. At His trial, they mocked His work as a prophet by daring Him to prophesy who had hit Him while He was blindfolded (Matthew 26:67-68). Yet He taught the people with unmistakeable authority, revealing to them the will of God for their salvation. All His parables, all His sermons, all His conversations with His disciples, and all the one-to-one discussions He had (with, for example, Nicodemus, or the woman of Samaria) were part of His prophetic work in His state of humiliation.

Priest. The whole of Christ's priestly work of satisfying divine justice was completed in His state of humiliation, when He lived His perfectly obedient life and died His atoning death. He also carried out His priestly work of intercession in this state too. As He told Peter, *"I have prayed for thee, that thy faith fail not"* (Luke 22:32).

King. While Christ was dying on the cross, He was mocked in His kingly role. *"He saved others; himself he cannot save. Let Christ the King of Israel descend now from the cross, that we may see and believe!"* (Mark 15:31-32) But it was actually there on the cross that He triumphantly conquered death and the devil. There too, He powerfully subdued the thief to Himself, winning his hard heart to acknowledge Him as Lord and giving him a desire to belong to His kingdom. He authoritatively assured the penitent thief that he was safe under His care. ***"Today, shalt thou be with me in paradise"*** (Luke 23:43).

Why did Christ humble Himself?

Once Christ had consented to be the Redeemer, He needed to be lowered to the place where He could bear sin, obey, suffer, and die. Christ had to humble Himself because of the terms of the covenant of grace.

But why did Christ agree to be the Redeemer, knowing all the humiliation it would involve? What could explain His willingness to take on this work? Part of the reason is that He loved His Father. When the Father purposed to save some people, the Son was delighted with this plan, even though it would cost Him dear. ***"Then said I, Lo, I come: in the volume of the book it is written of me, I delight to do thy will, O my God"*** (Psalm 40:7-8).

Part of the reason is also that Christ loved His people. The Father loved them, and Christ loved them. He delighted in them from everlasting (see Proverbs 8:22-31). Then, ***"having loved his own which were in the world, he loved them unto the end"*** (John 13:1). The Lord of glory came from incomprehensible heights and sank to unfathomable depths, and it was for love.

⚲ Something to think about...

- All the details of Christ's humiliation give incentives for us to love Him. Take a couple of examples from Question 27 and explain how they display Christ's loveliness.
- The Catechism lists different aspects of Christ's humiliation in roughly chronological order. Is this is also the order of least to worst humiliation?

Personal reflection
How far will you go for someone you love? If you love the Lord, how much will you put up with for His sake?

How was Christ highly exalted?

We have just studied the humiliation of Christ. We move on now to consider His exaltation. Humiliation involved Christ coming down from a high position. Exaltation is the reverse of that; it is His going from a low to a high position. Question 28 presents the exaltation of the Lord in four stages.

> **28** Wherein consisteth Christ's exaltation?
>
> Christ's exaltation consisteth in his rising again from the dead on the third day, in ascending up into heaven, in sitting at the right hand of God the Father, and in coming to judge the world at the last day.

Christ rose again

The resurrection is a historical fact. On the third day, Christ rose from the dead. He rose with the very same body in which He had suffered. The disciples saw Him. Initially they were terrified, thinking it was a ghost, but He reassured them it was really Him (see Luke 24:37-39).

"[The resurrection] shows that Christ is Lord of the living and the dead."

How was His resurrection part of His exaltation? For one thing, it honoured His body, which had suffered so much. It was the very same body as to its identity, but it was now incorruptible (not going to decay), glorious (with a heavenly splendour), powerful, and spiritual (a perfect instrument of the spirit).

More than this, it displayed the success of His work. It showed that He was the Son of God with power. It proved that He had fully satisfied God's justice for His people. It demonstrated that He had conquered death and the devil. And it shows that He is Lord of the living and the dead.

The doctrine of Christ's resurrection is very precious to the Christian and very important to the church. It is central to the gospel, for as Paul stated, *"If Christ be not raised, your faith is vain; ye are yet in your sins"* (1 Corinthians 15:17).

Christ ascended

Forty days after the resurrection, the Lord ascended up to heaven. He led the disciples out to Bethany and as He blessed them He was carried up before their eyes until at last a cloud took Him out of their sight (Luke 24:50-51).

Christ was exalted in the visible aspects of His ascension. The disciples, who had seen their Lord mocked, ill-treated and crucified, now saw Him before their very eyes being received up into the highest heavens.

Christ was also exalted in the invisible aspects of His ascension. The eyes of the disciples could not follow Him beyond the cloud, but they could know from Scripture some of what happened once He was out of eyesight. Christ the victorious Redeemer was received into glory, into the presence of His Father (Daniel 7:13-14, John 14:2), triumphing over all His enemies (Ephesians 4:8), to shouts of joy and praise from the angels (Psalm 24:7-10, Psalm 68:18).

Christ sits in heaven

In heaven Christ is advanced to the highest possible honour and dignity. He is positioned *"at the right hand of God the Father."* This is a metaphorical description of the highest place in heaven next to God the Father. As God, Christ is fully equal to the Father in all things. As the God-man, He is exalted to the highest place in heaven next to God.

Christ is exalted by *"sitting"* at the right hand of the Father. He sits, at rest, having successfully completed His work. He sits, continuing in this position of honour and authority. He sits, enjoying fullness of joy and pleasures for evermore.

Christ is exalted in the *work* He does at the Father's right hand. When Stephen got a glimpse of Christ in His exaltation, he saw Jesus standing (Acts 7:55-56) and in Revelation Jesus refers to Himself as the One who is walking in the midst of His church (Revelation 2:1). All these terms, 'sitting' and 'standing' and 'walking,' are metaphors, teaching us slightly different things. It is as if Christ is constantly stepping in to help His people. He is wielding all power in heaven and earth for them. In fact, as Question 23 told us, in His state of exaltation He is still carrying out His roles as prophet, priest, and king.

Christ will come again

Some of Christ's exaltation has taken place already (when He rose from the dead and ascended into heaven), and some is ongoing at the moment (His sitting in heaven). But there is even more exaltation to come in the future. Christ will come to judge the world at the last day.

God the Father has appointed a day, in which He will judge the world in righteousness. He will do this by *"that man whom he hath ordained"* (Acts 17:31), that is, Christ.

Several hundred people saw Jesus after He had risen from the dead. But at the last day, every eye shall see Him. This will be a display, in front of everyone who has ever lived, of the glory of the Redeemer.

Everyone who has ever lived will see and hear Him coming. It will be a most glorious event. He will descend from heaven with an arresting shout, with the voice of an archangel, and with the trumpet of God. He will come in His own glory, and in the glory of His Father, and with all the holy angels.

Everyone who has ever lived will be judged on this day. The Redeemer will judge the whole human race. There will be no possibility of avoiding this judgment, of escaping it, delaying it, or ignoring the summons. It will be obvious that Christ has both the right and the skills to do this work of judgment. He is omniscient, so He knows everything about everyone and their doings. He is omnipotent, so He has

> "In heaven Christ is advanced to the highest possible honour and dignity."

the power to summon them and then to send them, body and soul, either to heaven or hell. He is righteous, so He will dispense to everyone exactly what they deserve with absolute justice.

Because Christ humbled Himself, and completed the work the Father gave Him to do, therefore God has exalted Him, *"that at the name of Jesus, every knee should bow,... and that every tongue should confess that Jesus Christ is Lord, to the glory of God the Father"* (Philippians 2:10-11). Then the end will come, when Christ will deliver up the kingdom to His Father, and *"God...[will] be all in all"* (1 Corinthians 15:24-28).

Christ **exalted**

How does Christ carry out His offices of prophet, priest, and king in His state of exaltation?

Prophet
Christ has won the right to send the Spirit to apply the truth of His Word to save and sanctify His people. The Spirit ordinarily does this now through Christ's ministers, the ones who Christ sends out to preach His Word in His exalted name. *"When he ascended up on high, he ... gave gifts unto men ... He gave some, apostles; and some, prophets; and some, evangelists; and some, pastors and teachers..."* (Ephesians 4:8-11)

Priest
Christ's priestly work of satisfaction was completed once for all time in His state of humiliation. But His priestly work of intercession is ongoing in His state of exaltation. He stands in all His glory interceding for His people. For each in turn, He first removes their guilt and then grants daily supplies of grace. *"Who is he that condemneth? It is Christ that died, yea rather, that is risen again, who is even at the right hand of God, who also maketh intercession for us"* (Romans 8:34).

King
Christ in His state of exaltation sits on His throne managing the whole of providence for the welfare of His people. He arranges everything so that His people will unfailingly be brought into His kingdom and kept safe inside it. *For he must reign, till he hath put all enemies under his feet"* (1 Corinthians 15:25).

"Christ has won the right to send the Spirit to apply the truth of His Word to save and sanctify His people."

Q Something to think about...

- Paul says our preaching and our faith are useless and pointless if Christ did not rise from the dead (1 Corinthians 15:13-14). What does he mean?
- Have a look at Hebrews 1:1-3, which tells us what Christ is doing these days, in His exalted state. How many aspects of Christ's work as prophet, priest, and king can you find mentioned there?

Personal reflection

Those who are alive in Christ should set their hearts and minds on the things which are above, where Christ is sitting (Colossians 3:1-2). Do you ever think of where Christ is now and what He is doing? How would it help us to live as Christians if we focused more on these things?

We must all appear before the judgment seat of Christ. This is a terrifying thought for the enemies of Christ but Christ's people see it as even more reason to worship Him. What is your reaction to the prospect of the judgment?

How do we possess what Christ has purchased?

Question 29 opens a major new section in the Shorter Catechism. So far, we have seen why we need salvation (Questions 13-19) and we have seen what Christ has done in order to save us (Questions 20-28).

However the fact that Christ has suffered and died and risen again is not, in and of itself, all that is necessary for our salvation. If we are ill, we will not be cured simply by the fact that there is a remedy available. It will not do to simply imagine that the doctor could cure us or that the hospital could treat our condition. We must actually visit the doctor, receive the treatment, and take the medicine, if we wish to get better. In the same way it is not enough for us to know that there is a cure for the disease of sin and that others have been saved. We ourselves must receive this salvation.

Question 29 begins to explain how we get the benefit of Christ's redeeming work. Questions 30-31 will explain how we are united to Christ. Then we will look at the blessings this brings us, both in this life (Questions 32-36) and in the future (Questions 37 and 38).

> **29** How are we made partakers of the redemption purchased by Christ?
>
> We are made partakers of the redemption purchased by Christ, by the effectual application of it to us by his Holy Spirit.

We need the Holy Spirit

So far, the Catechism has told us what the Father and the Son have done towards our redemption. God the Father purposed it (Question 20). God the Son purchased it (Questions 21-28). Now, God the Holy Spirit applies it.

> "Everyone who the Son purchased salvation for, the Spirit will apply it to."

There is an exact correlation between the work of the three persons of the Trinity. Everyone who the Father purposed to save, the Son purchased salvation for (and nobody else). Everyone who the Son purchased salvation for, the Spirit will apply it to (and nobody else). If we are going to be saved at all, we need the Spirit as much as we need the Father and the Son.

To 'apply' redemption to someone means: to give it to them, to deliver it to them personally, to put them in possession of it, to make it theirs. We talk about applying sun cream—taking it out of the bottle and actually spreading it on your skin; or applying a bandage—unrolling it and actually wrapping it round the injured limb. Whatever Christ has purchased for sinners (for example, an understanding of His truth, cleansing from sin, a place in His kingdom), the Spirit actually puts those sinners in personal possession of it. The Holy Spirit applies redemption 'effectually,' or effectively. You might apply sunscreen but not everywhere it is needed. Or you might apply a bandage too loosely or too tightly. These applications would therefore not be effective. But the Holy Spirit never fails in His work. He is always effective. Whenever He sets out to teach someone the truth, cleanse someone from sin, or bring them into Christ's kingdom (for example), they are actually taught, actually cleansed, actually brought.

We need to be **made partakers**

Despite the complete salvation which is perfectly readily available, and despite our desperate need of salvation, we are unable to apply redemption to ourselves. We are too sinful and too weak. We sit in church and hear about salvation, and we read our Bibles and understand what salvation is available, yet have no ability to go and partake of it. In fact, we are too sinful to even want to partake of it. We never desire salvation but rather fight against it. This is why we have to be *"made partakers."* We won't and we can't take possession of salvation for ourselves. The Holy Spirit has to actually give it to us. In salvation we are utterly dependent on the radical, life-giving and enabling power of the Holy Spirit.

"In salvation we are utterly dependent on the radical, life-giving and enabling power of the Holy Spirit."

⌕ Something to think about...

- Sinners have salvation within their reach. Whose fault is it if they don't seek the Saviour?
- Sinners depend on the Holy Spirit to put them in actual possession of salvation. Who deserves the credit when sinners are saved?

How do we receive redemption?

We have just seen in Question 29 that we need the Holy Spirit to apply to us the redemption which Christ has purchased. Question 30 explains how He does this. It tackles two points. How does the Spirit actually apply redemption? By uniting us to Christ in our effectual calling. And how does He do that? By working faith in us.

> **30** How does the Spirit apply to us the redemption purchased by Christ?
>
> The Spirit applieth to us the redemption purchased by Christ, by working faith in us, and thereby uniting us to Christ in our effectual calling.

The Spirit unites us to Christ

In order to get the benefit of the redemption Christ has purchased, we need to be united to Christ. We need to make contact with Christ; we need to be attached to Christ; we need to be made one with Christ.

> "Christ's people are like the limbs of a body and Christ is the head."

As fallen sinners, we have no relationship to the Redeemer; and indeed we have no power and no inclination to have anything to do with Him. If we are going to begin to know Christ, or have any connection with Christ in a saving way, it is the Spirit who has to do the work. As we will see in Question 31, the way the Spirit does this work is by giving us an the Spirit does this work by an *"effectual calling."* For now, we will focus on the union which He creates between Christ and the soul.

This union is a unique kind of one-ness between Christ and His people. It is illustrated in Scripture in various ways: Christ's people are like the limbs of a body and Christ is the head; Christ's people are like the spouse in a marriage and Christ is the husband; Christ's people are like the branches of a vine and Christ is the vine itself; Christ's people are like the bricks in a building and Christ is the foundation; Christ's people are like someone eating and drinking, and Christ is the food and the drink. We have to take the main idea from each of these illustrations and join them together to get some picture of what union with Christ is like. It is a union where Christ is 'in us' and at the same time we are 'in Christ,' a relationship of incomparable closeness, interdependence, and love; it is beyond description.

This union is formed for each of Christ's people personally at a point in time in their lifetime. It is sometimes called the 'mystical union'. There is a sense in which Christ's people have always been united to Him - in what is sometimes called the federal union, when God purposed to save them in Christ in past eternity, and Christ represented them in all His work of redemption. But until the purposed and purchased redemption is actually applied to a sinner, they remain in their fallen state of sin and misery, estranged from Christ and enemies of Christ. The Holy Spirit unites them to Christ, each one personally or subjectively in their individual experience, in their own individual *"effectual calling."*

The Spirit gives us faith

The Spirit applies the redemption which Christ has purchased by *"uniting us to Christ in our effectual calling."* But how does He do this? What means does He use? His means of uniting us to Christ is *"by working faith in us."* Giving us faith is the means, uniting us to Christ is the result.

One of the most common ways of referring to those who are saved is by calling them *'believers,'* that is, those who have faith. But nobody has faith of their own accord. Our faith is *"not of ourselves: it is the gift of God"* (Ephesians 2:8), and specifically, it is the gift of God the Holy Spirit. If we are believers, it is because we have been made believers by the Holy Spirit.

The Spirit produces faith in a soul by bringing the soul from spiritual death to spiritual life. Until the Spirit works, the soul is dead in trespasses and sins. It takes the almighty power of God the Holy Spirit to bring a dead soul to life. He normally does so in the context of the Word. He surrounds the soul with the truth about Christ which is made known in the Word. As soon as the Spirit makes the soul spiritually alive, the soul believes in Christ — the very same Christ who is revealed in the Word. Faith is how we make contact with Christ, the connecting link between us and the Saviour.

The faith which the Spirit produces is *faith in Christ*. It is not a vague religious feeling. It is not an ignorant acceptance of things we don't understand. Faith is grasping hold of Christ, reaching and receiving the Saviour, so that we are made one with the Redeemer. Faith unites us to Christ who has purchased the redemption which the Spirit is now applying. We cannot produce saving faith in ourselves. But Spirit-produced faith is Christ-grasping faith. The faith the Spirit produces is faith that unites us to Christ.

⌕ Something to think about...

- Look back at the illustrations given above of union with Christ. What are the main ideas of each illustration? What do they show us about this union? Here are some Scripture references: Body/head - Ephesians 4:15-16; Wife/husband - Ephesians 5:29-32; Branches/vine -John 15:1-7; Bricks/foundation - 1 Peter 2:4-6; Eating and drinking/food and drink - John 6:53-57. Can you find other references and/or other illustrations?
- If God has purposed to save us, and Christ has completely redeemed us, why do we need faith?

Personal reflection

What is your self-identity? Paul described himself as *'a man in Christ.'* Is this how you would like to think of yourself? If you are a Christian, how does the fact that you are *'in Christ'* shape your identity as *'a believer'*?

What is effectual calling?

Question 31 gets to the meat of the application of redemption. We have seen in Question 29 that we need the Holy Spirit to apply redemption. Then Question 30 explained that we need to be united to Christ. Union with Christ requires faith, on our part. Additionally, as Question 31 now teaches, there needs to be "effectual calling," on the Spirit's part. So, what is effectual calling?

31 What is effectual calling?

Effectual calling is the work of God's Spirit, whereby, convincing us of our sin and misery, enlightening our minds in the knowledge of Christ, and renewing our wills, he doth persuade and enable us to embrace Jesus Christ, freely offered to us in the gospel.

The Spirit's call

A universal call

There is a call that goes out to everyone who hears the gospel. It calls you, whoever you are, to receive Jesus Christ as your own Saviour. This call is universal. It goes out to everyone, whatever their age, gender, ethnicity, or social status. It goes out to the lost, the foolish, those who mock at God, flagrant transgressors, those who are far from righteousness, the rebellious, those who have sinned to their uttermost, the conceited, and those who are unaware of their sinfulness and misery.

A free offer

By this call, Jesus Christ is *"freely offered to us in the gospel."* He is *"freely offered"*:

- as a gift, without money and without price. There are no conditions you need to meet, or qualifications you need to bring.
- indiscriminately, to anyone who hears. It doesn't matter what kind

> "Nobody needs to remain unaware of who Christ is and what He has done."

of sinner you have been or how sinful you are.

Christ is *"freely offered"*:

- He is announced and displayed. The message is crystal clear. The picture is full colour in high definition. Christ is presented in all His glory for all to see. Nobody needs to remain unaware of who Christ is and what He has done.
- He is recommended and made available. This gift is held out to us. Christ is put within our reach. He is proposed and proffered and urged on us. We are made welcome to receive Him. Nobody needs to go away without taking possession of Christ for themselves.

An effectual **call**

Many, many people have heard the universal call and it leaves them cold. They hear it, but they don't respond. As far as their salvation is concerned, the universal call was ineffectual.

But when the Spirit is applying redemption, He makes the universal call an effectual call. He makes something happen so that it becomes more than words and syllables and facts and ideas. When the Spirit accompanies the universal call, he gives it the power to strike home in the person's heart, so that they actually hear its authority and urgency, they actually recognise it as addressed to them personally, and they actually do what it says.

The sinner's **response**

When the Spirit effectually calls us to receive Christ, we actually do this. We respond by *"We respond by coming to "embrace Jesus Christ."* Christ is offered and we accept Him. Christ is freely offered, and we are delighted and thankful with this gift.

To *"embrace Jesus Christ"* is a way of describing faith. The faith that unites us to Christ is an embracing of Christ. It is warm-hearted — we are so pleased to discover Christ that we grasp him tightly to us and give ourselves over to Him. *"My Beloved is mine, and I am his"* (Song of Solomon 2:16). It is all-inclusive — we wrap our arms around the whole Christ, the God-man, our prophet, priest, and king, whether we think of Him in His humiliation or His exaltation. *"But of him are ye in Christ Jesus, who of God is made unto us wisdom, and righteousness, and sanctification, and redemption"* (1 Corinthians 1:30).

The Spirit **helps us to respond**

Although Christ is a complete Saviour and an available Saviour, we need to be made willing and made able to embrace Him. This persuading and enabling is done by the Holy Spirit.

How does He do this? Viewed from one perspective, the Spirit acts instantaneously. There was a moment in time when we stopped being spiritually dead and became spiritually alive. This was the moment of regeneration, the moment when we were born again, the moment when the Spirit gave us the new birth. Seen in this way, the effectual call is like a court summons, brought to you with a knock on the door by officers who take you there straight away. Or it is like the starting gun in a race, instantly compelling the runners into action. At that moment, the soul is summoned from death to life and instantly embraces Christ.

Viewed from another perspective, the Holy Spirit uses a process. He works gradually, over a period of time. This is like the process of turning a huge container ship round from sailing south to sailing north, or the process of heating up a liquid until it reaches boiling point. When the Catechism speaks of the Spirit working by *"convincing us ... enlightening our minds ... and renewing our wills,"* it lets us think of effectual calling as a process. Nevertheless it is a process with a definite end-point. Although there is movement, you don't say the ship has turned until it is facing due north. Although the temperature rises, you don't say water has boiled until it reaches exactly 100°C. The process of effectual calling is actually completed at the point where the soul is made alive. Just at the point when the light finally penetrates their mind and their will is turned to choose holiness, the sinner embraces Jesus Christ.

The Spirit convinces

We already know the facts about our sinfulness and our misery (Questions 17-19). But when the Spirit convinces us, these facts take on a vivid, personal reality. Now the sinner realises, *'I am a sinner, I am lacking in righteousness and full of corruption, I am constantly sinning, and I am unworthy and guilty.'* The sinner feels that God is righteous to be angry with them. The sinner feels their misery, that life is wrong and empty without Christ. They feel that the wrath and curse of God is only what they deserve.

"The conviction of sin brings people to ask with real urgency, 'What must I do to be saved?'"

The conviction of sin brings people to ask with real urgency, **"What must I do to be saved?"** (Acts 16:30) But conviction of sin is not salvation. The Spirit must continue to work in the heart of the sinner.

The Spirit enlightens

The Spirit works *"enlightening our minds in the knowledge of Christ."* We already know the facts about who Christ is and His work of redemption (Questions 21-28). But when the Spirit enlightens us, we see the personal implications of Christ's work for ourselves. The Spirit shows us that: Christ is *able* to save *me*; He is *willing* to save *me*; He is *faithful* to save *me*; He is *exactly suited* to the need *I* have of salvation. For the first time, we begin to appreciate the work that Christ has done - to purchase salvation as our priest, to make salvation known as our prophet, and to give effect to salvation as our king. The Spirit makes plain to us that Christ is the way of salvation. The light of this truth was always shining, but the Spirit gives us eyesight to see its brightness. Now we see Christ as totally worthy of our devotion and totally worthy of our trust.

The Spirit renews

The Spirit works *"renewing our wills."* Our will always acts in accordance with what kind of person we are. If we are fallen, our wills choose against God and away from Christ. **"Ye will not (i.e., you are not willing to) come to me that ye might have life"** (John 5:40). God never forces anyone to do anything against their will. Christ has no unwilling converts. What the Holy Spirit does is to *renew* the will. When He changes what kind of person we are, from spiritually dead to spiritually alive, our will changes direction so that we lose our aversion to God and our disinclination to religious things. We now choose God and decide in favour of Christ and incline towards what is holy and good. **"Thy people shall be willing in the day of thy power"** (Psalm 110:3).

🔍 Something to think about...

- Anyone can find out the facts about who Jesus is and how Jesus saves. Why do people who know it all, still refuse to believe?
- If it was entirely up to us to choose, would anyone ever be saved?

Personal reflection

When Christ calls, *"Look unto me, and be ye saved"* what do you hear? A far-away voice that can't quite get through the noise generated by your own sin and worldliness? A message for someone else? An offer that you half-suspect might be a scam? Or the voice of your beloved, your Lord and Redeemer?

What are the benefits of salvation?

Question 32 opens a new section in the Shorter Catechism. So far, we have seen what God does in salvation. Now we turn in Questions 32 to 38 to look at what God gives us when He saves us. The blessings of salvation are many and vast. God does all the work, and we get all the benefit.

> **32** What benefits do they that are effectually called partake of in this life?
>
> They that are effectually called do in this life partake of justification, adoption and sanctification, and the several benefits which, in this life, do either accompany or flow from them.

Real benefits

Some people scoff at Christians and say they lead gloomy, miserable lives. If we were to ask such people what advantage there is to being a Christian, they would probably say none at all. They look at all the things they enjoy which Christians can't and won't do, and think that Christians disadvantage themselves by their needless, pointless self-denial. And Christians are often disadvantaged in the world by the prejudice and oppression of unbelievers.

But those who the Spirit has called into union with Christ experience real blessings, deep and rich blessings, which far surpass any benefits that we receive from the poor, passing things of this world.

Justification, adoption and sanctification are real solutions to real problems. As we have to take a holistic view of our sin - it affects every part of us and every aspect of our relation to God - so we have to take a holistic view of our salvation. We are really saved, in every possible way. We are blessed in our status before God, in our relationship with God, and in every part of our soul and body.

"real blessings, deep and rich blessings, which far surpass any benefits ... of this world"

Justification, adoption and sanctification are blessings in themselves and they bring further blessings along with them. No wonder then that David said, *"Thou hast put gladness in my heart, more than in the time that their corn and their wine increased"* (Psalm 4:7).

Spiritual benefits

There is always a danger that the church, as it works and witnesses in this world, will focus too much of its energies on trying to help people improve their circumstances in life. This can lead to the church becoming viewed as a sort of social work organisation whose aim and purpose is to make people's lives more tolerable here in this world. It is, of course, very important that we help people by alleviating pain and suffering wherever we can.

At the same time it is crucial that we never lose sight of the fact that people's biggest problems are spiritual. As the gospel is primarily concerned with people's spiritual problems, correspondingly the benefits that come with the gospel are first and foremost spiritual.

Present benefits

There is a common misunderstanding about the gospel, that all its benefits belong to heaven. According to this view, Christians have no particular blessings in this world and have to wait until they die to get any good from their faith.

This is completely wrong. As we are surrounded with spiritual problems here and now, the gospel gives us solutions for these problems here and now. Our lives are transformed now as we begin to enjoy union with Christ. Now, instantly, and for the duration of our lives, we enjoy the blessings of justification, adoption and sanctification, and the additional blessings associated with them. We will look in more detail at these in Questions 33-36.

An old minister in Scotland was once very ill. A friend visited him asked him if he thought he was dying. The old man answered, "Really, friend, I do not care whether I am or no; if I die I shall be with God, and if I live God shall be with me."

Future benefits

While there are many benefits which reach us in this life, there are more to come. In Questions 37 and 38 we will look at the benefits we receive at death and at the last day. It is undoubtedly the case that the full enjoyment of the blessings of salvation is reserved for heaven. We get a sample and a preview in this life, and the complete blessedness in the life to come. This is what David looked forward to: *"In thy presence is fullness of joy; at thy right hand there are pleasures for evermore"* (Psalm 16:11).

"the most comfortable and pleasant life that any one can ever live in this world"

ℚ **Something to think about...**

Personal reflection
According to Matthew Henry, the seventeenth century Bible commentator, *"A holy heavenly life spent in the service of God, and in communion with Him, is, without doubt, the most pleasant and comfortable life any man can live in this world."* Do you agree with him?

How are sinners justified?

When Question 32 began to list the blessings that believers enjoy in this life, justification was top of the list. It is critically important to get the doctrine of justification right. Where the doctrine of justification stands, the church stands; where this doctrine collapses, the church collapses. So, much of our peace and comfort as believers comes from an accurate understanding of justification.

---

33 What is justification?

Justification is an act of God's free grace, wherein he pardoneth all our sins, and accepteth us as righteous in his sight, only for the righteousness of Christ imputed to us, and received by faith alone.

Justification is **pardon and acceptance**

"God justifies us *only* because of Christ's righteousness imputed to us."

The blessing of justification has two components - one is that God pardons all our sins, and the other is that God accepts us as righteous in His sight.

When God **"pardons all our sins,"** He removes all our guilt and releases us from the curse of the broken law. Whatever debt we owed God by our sins, God now regards as having been paid for us.

When God **"accepts us as righteous,"** He brings us into His favour and entitles us to eternal life. Whatever duty we were required to give God by way of obedience, God now regards as having been provided for us.

In justification, God acts towards us as a judge. He pronounces a sentence referring to our legal status. Before we are justified, our legal status is *condemned* — we are guilty and deserve death. But now, our legal status is *justified* — we are pardoned and entitled to life.

Justification is **on the basis of Christ's righteousness**

When God pronounces the sentence of justification on a sinner, how does it reflect reality? Since these sinners are undeniably guilty, is it just a legal fiction when God calls them *'not guilty'*?

God's judgments are never contrary to fact. When he says someone is *'not guilty,'* they are in reality not guilty. The sentence of justification is appropriate because of the righteousness of Christ imputed to us.

If someone imputes something to you they are assigning it to your account, or crediting you with it. God imputes Christ's righteousness to His people. He credits them with Christ's righteousness, or assigns it to them. In law, Christ's righteousness becomes theirs. So now they deserve all that Christ's righteousness deserves.

Christ's righteousness has two components - He paid the penalty of the broken law (by His sufferings and death) and He gave all the obedience due to the law (by His perfect life). Both these components are attributed to His people in justification. Because Christ paid the penalty, His people are pardoned. Because Christ gave perfect obedience, His people are accepted. God pronounces them justified because, in possession of Christ's righteousness, they are truly legally righteous.

God does not justify us because of our own righteousness, but because of Christ's. Nor does God justify us partly because of a righteousness imputed to us from outside and partly because of a righteousness intrinsically residing inside us. God justifies us *only* because of Christ's righteousness imputed to us.

Justification is **by faith alone**

How do we receive the righteousness of Christ? By faith in Christ. What then is the role of faith in justification? How does faith justify us?

- Not as if faith is an act or a work that deserves justification as a reward.
- Not as if faith will do in the place of obedience, as if God lets us off without a perfect righteousness as long as we can believe.
- Not as if justification is a reward for the graces (such as love) that accompany faith or any good works that spring from faith.

Instead, faith justifies us only in the sense that faith is the *instrument* which receives Christ and His righteousness. We speak of spoon-feeding a baby. But the baby feeds from the spoon only in the sense that the spoon is the instrument which delivers the actual food. Faith justifies us only in the same sense as a spoon feeds us. It is not *our work of receiving* Christ's righteousness that justifies us, but *Christ's righteousness itself.*

Saying that faith is merely an instrument does not undermine the necessity for faith. We are not justified until we believe. Until we believe in Christ, we remain in a state of condemnation, still guilty, and still deserving death. This is notwithstanding the fact that God has invincibly purposed to save us from all eternity, and the fact that Christ has triumphantly secured our salvation by His work of redemption. Until the sinner actually believes, they are not justified.

Justification is **an act**

Justification is an act. This means that it is completed all at once, at a moment in time. It is not something that happens over a period of time.

Justification is *"an act of God."* We cannot justify ourselves. We cannot be justified by the church. It is exclusively God who justifies us.

Justification is a *judicial* act of God. It is something God does as a judge in a court of law. He pronounces a sentence, or gives a verdict. This verdict is delivered once and once only. It is not possible to be justified again and again. Nor is it possible for justification to be altered or reversed.

Justification is **by free grace**

Justification is an act *"of God's free grace."* We can see this from several different angles.

- God could have refused to justify us unless we had provided our own perfect satisfaction to His justice. But instead He accepts the righteousness of Christ on our behalf.
- God Himself sent Christ to provide this righteousness on our behalf.
- God requires nothing on our part for justification apart from faith, and this faith is itself His gift.
- God does not look for anything in the sinner to influence Him to justify them, or to deserve His favour.

> "Justification by God's free grace removes every opportunity for us to boast about ourselves."

Justification by God's free grace removes every opportunity for us to boast about ourselves. It gives all the glory to God alone.

🔍 Something to think about...

- How do the two components of Christ's righteousness match up with the two components of our justification?
- *'If you don't believe, you can't be justified.'* Does this mean that God depends on our faith in order to justify us? What is the connection between faith and justification?

How are sinners adopted?

If we have been called into union with Christ, then as well as being justified we are also adopted. If you adopt a child, you take them into your family and bring them up as your own. The child becomes, in love and in law, a full member of your family.

> **What is adoption?**
>
> Adoption is an act of God's free grace, whereby we are received into the number, and have a right to all the privileges of the sons of God.

Is adoption desirable?

As sinners we find ourselves orphans, rejected and abandoned.

Who can look after us? Adam only bequeathed us a legacy of sinfulness and misery. He has no resources to help us any more. We are too much responsibility for him now.

Who will take us in? Satan is the one we seem to most resemble in our character and behaviour (see 1 John 3:8-10). But Satan will only use and abuse us as slaves. He has no interest in our welfare however much we take after him.

When you think of this family background, adoption by God becomes very desirable. To be included as one of the number of a much-

> "To be included as one of the number of a much-loved family, and to have God as our own Father, is surely something we should want to have for ourselves."

loved family, and to have God as our own Father, is surely something we should want to have for ourselves. What then are some of the privileges that we are given a right to, when God adopts us?

God provides for His children
The Lord gives good things to everyone, whether or not they are His children. However, only His children receive these things from His love, as special personal gifts from their Father in heaven. Others receive them by His leave, not with His love.

God teaches His children
God brings up His children gently and kindly in the right way, teaching them to walk to start with (Hosea 11:3) and giving them good advice about all aspects of life (Proverbs). When they go astray, He disciplines them in love, bringing them back on the right track and back into closeness with Himself.

God gives His children the family likeness

When parents adopt a child they give them the family name, but they can't give them a family likeness. But God's adopted children take after their Father. They are not only 'Christian' in name, but 'Christ-like' in nature. Their new heart grows up in their Father's image, after His likeness, as they are increasingly conformed to Christ, their elder brother.

God protects His children

There is nothing more natural than for a child, sensing danger, to seek the protection of their parents. The Lord protects His children with infinite tenderness and pity (Psalm 103:13-14). He is all knowing; no problem arises that He is unaware of. He is all-powerful; no problem arises that He is unable to deal with. From natural and spiritual enemies He keeps His children safe and secure (Psalm 91).

God listens to His children

Sometimes parents are unable to hear their children. God is always able to hear His children and welcomes them at all times into His presence. He is never too busy or too tired to pay attention to their hopes and fears.

God takes His children home

At the end of their lives, God takes His children home to heaven. There He gives them their full inheritance. They are *"heirs of God and joint-heirs with Christ"* (Romans 8:17), due to inherit everything that Christ inherits, in the home He has prepared for them.

> "God is not adopting a needy child or even a stranger's child into His family. He is adopting His enemies, those who hate Him and all His ways."

Is adoption deserved?

Adoption is an *"act of God's free grace."* It is an act in the sense that it is done all at once at a moment in time (in fact, at the same moment as justification). How does adoption display God's free grace?

- There was nothing attractive about us. Parents might adopt a child because they fall in love with her looks and affectionate disposition. But we are disfigured and diseased by sin, and we will need constant care and attention for the rest of our lives. God loves us and takes us on in spite of this.
- We didn't deserve it. We were not only pitiful, but hateful. God is not adopting a needy child or even a stranger's child into His family. He is adopting His enemies, those who hate Him and all His ways.
- God didn't need us. He already had His own, only begotten, beloved Son, who He was entirely pleased with and who completely loved Him.
- God had to go to great lengths to adopt us. Parents have to go through an elaborate process involving many administrative hurdles before they can adopt a child. God gave His only begotten Son to suffer and die.
- Justification is already a huge blessing. Adoption is even greater. It would have been wonderful grace if God had only been reconciled to us. It is even more wonderful that God counts us as His dear children and lavishes on us all the privileges of belonging to His family.

🔍 Something to think about...

- If someone doesn't belong to God's family, whose family do they belong to?
- What does God do for His children?
- John marvelled, ***"Behold what manner of love the Father hath bestowed upon us, that we should be called the sons of God"*** (1 John 3:1). What is so marvellous about God's love in adopting?

How are sinners made holy?

We have seen in Questions 33 and 34 the blessings of justification and adoption which God provides for us when we are called into union with Christ. Now in Question 35 we turn to look at a blessing which God produces in us - the blessing of sanctification.

35 What is sanctification?

Sanctification is the work of God's free grace, whereby we are renewed in the whole man after the image of God, and are enabled more and more to die unto sin, and live unto righteousness.

Sanctification is an **ongoing work**

Sanctification is *"the work of God's free grace."* Unlike justification and adoption, which are *"acts,"* completed all at once, sanctification is a *"work,"* or a process, which takes place gradually. Although God begins the work of sanctification at precisely the same moment in time as He justifies and adopts the sinner, God continues the process of sanctification over a period of time - in fact, for the rest of the person's life.

The work of sanctification is done out of God's love and rich mercy. It is the work of God, and the special work of God the Holy Spirit.

> "The person being sanctified increasingly dies to sin."

Sanctification is a **renewing work**

When God sanctifies us, He *"renews us."* He gives us a new nature, or implants new life in us, or infuses grace into us. This renewal is not a case of polishing up what was there before, because what was there before was only corruption and pollution. Instead God gives us an entirely new nature - new understanding in our mind, new inclinations in our will, new loves and loathings, and new ways of behaving.

Originally, we were made in the image of God, in knowledge, righteousness and holiness (as we saw in Question 10). But we lost these aspects of the image of God in the fall. When God sanctifies us, He begins to restore this lost image. We are renewed *"after the image of God,"* in knowledge (Colossians 3:10) and in righteousness and holiness (Ephesians 4:24).

Although God renews us *"in the whole man,"* this does not mean we are wholly renewed. We have real light in our minds, for example, but some darkness remains. We have real inclinations towards holiness in our wills, but also some remaining strong desires after sin. We have real love for Christ, but also some continuing love for self and sin. Sanctification reaches to every part of us, but it is not complete in every part. We will not be wholly sanctified until we reach heaven.

Sanctification is **an enabling work**

When God sanctifies us, we *"are enabled more and more to die unto sin and live unto righteousness."*

The person being sanctified *increasingly dies to sin*. This means hating our own sin, fighting against our own sin, rooting out our sinful tendencies, acts, words and thoughts. At the same time, the person being sanctified *increasingly lives to righteousness*. This means loving holiness and practicing holiness by righteous ways of thinking and behaving.

God the Holy Spirit is the one who enables us to grow in grace. Nevertheless, we are the ones who grow. In sanctification we have to be active. We have to fight against our sin and we have to lead holy lives. This is in contrast to justification and adoption, where we are completely passive and God does everything. In justification God pronounces the sentence and in adoption God transfers us into His family, and we simply receive the effects of God's acts. However, in sanctification, we strive, labour, self-discipline, walk, battle, and bear fruit. There is no possibility of us cooperating with God in our justification or adoption. But in sanctification, we do and must cooperate with God. *"Work out your own salvation with fear and trembling. For it is God which worketh in you both to will and to do of his good pleasure"* (Philippians 2:12-13).

Sanctification is a progressive work. We grow in grace. This growth is often unsteady, often imperceptible, and often regresses. Nevertheless the overall trend is *more and more* holiness. A Christian at the end of their life is overall more holy than when they were first regenerated, even though they are not as holy as they want to be, and even though their increased holiness is still tiny compared to perfection.

> "In sanctification, we strive, labour, self-discipline, walk, battle, and bear fruit."

🔍 Something to think about...

- *"Be not conformed to this world: but be ye transformed by the renewing of your mind"* (Romans 12:2). How is it possible for sinners to follow this advice? What does it look like in practice when someone is being sanctified?
- Often, as believers get older and come nearer the end of their lives, this is the time when they feel they are more sinful than ever before. Does this mean they haven't been sanctified?

Personal reflection

Do you aspire to grow in holiness? Do you think that fighting sin is worth the effort? Where do you turn for help to grow in grace?

What benefits accompany salvation?

In the last three chapters we have focussed on justification, adoption and sanctification. However these are not the only benefits of salvation. If God has pardoned and accepted us (in justification), included us among His children and granted us the privilege of His sons (in adoption) and begun the work of making us holy (in sanctification), then several other other precious blessings either accompany them or result from them.

> What are the benefits which in this life do accompany or flow from justification, adoption, and sanctification?

The benefits which in this life do accompany or flow from justification, adoption and sanctification are, assurance of God's love, peace of conscience, joy in the Holy Ghost, increase of grace, and perseverance therein to the end.

Assurance of God's love

"Assurance of God's love" is the certainty that God loves you. Before justification we can only be certain that we are under the wrath and curse of God. But justification shows how *"God commendeth his love toward us, in that, while we were yet sinners, Christ died for us"* (Romans 5:8). Adoption shows us the love of God in pitying and taking in a hopeless, rejected child (Ezekiel 16:1-14). Sanctification shows the love of God in so patiently and carefully drawing us on in His ways (Deuteronomy 32:10-12).

Peace of conscience

"Peace of conscience" is when you know that the accusations against you have an answer. If we are not united to Christ we can only have a troubled, disquieted conscience as we reflect on ourselves in the light of God's law and scrabble around for excuses. But justification means that our conscience is sprinkled with the blood of

"Adoption means that we do not need to live in fear like slaves."

Christ (Hebrews 10:22). Adoption means that we do not need to live in fear like slaves, because we have received the Spirit of adoption, by whom we cry, *"Abba, Father"* (Romans 8:15). Sanctification does not mean that we are perfect, but when we know we are genuinely pursuing holiness, our conscience has less to accuse us of. *"For our rejoicing is this, the testimony of our conscience, that in simplicity and godly sincerity ... we have had our conversation ..."* (2 Corinthians 1:12).

Joy in the Holy Ghost

"Joy in the Holy Ghost" is comfort and pleasure you find in God when the Spirit is in you and you are in Him.

Prior to the Spirit's work, the things that make us joyful are earthly and sinful, while the thought of God makes us uneasy and unhappy. But justification makes us rejoice and glory in God when we realise what huge blessings we possess by being pardoned and accepted. *"We also joy in God through our Lord Jesus Christ, by whom we have now received the atonement"* (Romans 5:11). Adoption gives us joy when we think of the goodness of our Father, the kindness of our elder Brother, and the fellowship of our Comforter, not to mention the riches at our disposal in His household and the inheritance of His children that awaits us. Sanctification gives us a joy in the Holy Ghost that can't be enjoyed when we fall into sin, as David discovered. *"Take not thy Holy Spirit from me. Restore unto me the joy of thy salvation"* (Psalm 51:11-12).

Increase of grace

"Increase of grace" means growing in all aspects of grace. Justification sets us free from our guilt so that we are in a position to serve God unreservedly from now on. Adoption makes us the kind of children who grow by the sincere milk of the Word (1 Peter 2:2). Sanctification is a progressive work which by definition must increase. *"The path of the just is as the shining light, that shineth more and more unto the perfect day"* (Proverbs 4:18).

Perseverance to the end

Perseverance in grace is continuing in the state of grace until the end of your life. Justification produces perseverance because God's pardon and acceptance can never be reversed. Jesus *"by his own blood ... obtained an eternal redemption for us"* (Hebrews 9:12). Adoption produces perseverance because God never disowns one of His children but will continue to bring them up in His family so that He will eventually put them in possession of their inheritance — eternal life. Sanctification produces perseverance because the Spirit who sanctifies us *"abide with you for ever"* (John 14:16), so that we grow up to full maturity in every way in Christ (Ephesians 4:13, 15).

> "Justification produces perseverance because God's pardon and acceptance can never be reversed."

🔍 Something to think about...

- Justification, adoption, and sanctification all come together as a package. When you open the package, all these other benefits have been included too. They are all inextricably linked. What does this tell us about the emptiness of someone's life if they are not saved?
- Imagine somebody who is always joyous and upbeat and whose conscience doesn't trouble them but who, instead of growing in grace, immerses themselves in a worldly and immoral lifestyle. Does this person possess the blessings of 'peace of conscience' and 'joy in the Holy Ghost' or do they have something different?
- Imagine somebody who is never persuaded that God loves them, always worried about their sins, and who always looks at the darker side of life. How would it help this person if they reconsidered what God has done in justification, adoption, and sanctification?

Can death bring a blessing?

Questions 32 to 26 have focussed our minds on the blessings which Christians enjoy in this life. These blessings cover every aspect of life. But the benefits of redemption do not simply refer to this life. There are more benefits to come. Question 37 deals with the blessings believers receive at death. There are two areas in which the Christian is blessed at death - in their soul and in their body.

37 What benefits do believers receive from Christ at death?

The souls of believers are at their death made perfect in holiness, and do immediately pass into glory; and their bodies, being still united to Christ, do rest in their graves till the resurrection.

Their souls are **made perfect**

For believers and unbelievers alike, death is the separation of soul and body. But there the similarity ends.

When a believer dies, their soul is made perfect in holiness. It is now perfectly free from all sin, and shall remain so for ever. They will have no more sinful thoughts, words or actions. Never again will they have to mourn over their sins. The believer's soul is also now made perfectly like Christ. This is what John looked forward to. **"We shall be like him; for we shall see him as he is"** (1 John 3:2).

But unbelievers die in their sins and go to a place where they do nothing but sin. Never again will they have the opportunity to embrace Christ as their Saviour from sin.

Their souls **enter glory**

As soon as the believer dies their soul goes to heaven. There they enter the presence of God and see God face to face. This is the essence of heaven, or what makes glory to be glory. They also enjoy the glorious

"Never again will they have to mourn over their sins."

company of the holy angels and the spirits of all the other believers who have died before.

This is the complete opposite of what happens to the soul of the unbeliever. Instead of glory, the unbeliever goes away into disgrace and punishment. They are consigned to the prison of hell and keep company with devils and all the other unbelievers who have died before.

The believer goes into glory **"immediately"** when they die. You remember how Christ assured the thief on the cross that he would be with Him in heaven **"today"** (Luke 24:43). There is no interval between the soul and the body being separated in death and the soul entering glory. A famous Scottish minister called Robert Bruce, the day he died, told his family, I have breakfasted with you, and shall sup with my Lord Jesus Christ this night.

Their bodies **are resting**

When the believer's soul goes to glory, what happens to their body? It is not forgotten or left behind.

Believers' bodies *"rest in their graves"*. The Bible often refers to this period as sleeping. For example, in Isaiah the believer in the grave is pictured as lying in his bed resting (Isaiah 57:2). They are no longer conscious of what is going on in the world, but they are safe and they are at peace. They are resting there *"till the resurrection."* Then they will be reunited with their souls and receive further blessing. Again, this is in complete contrast to what happens to the unbeliever. The unbeliever's body is kept in the grave as in a prison, reserved for judgment.

Their bodies **are united to Christ**

The believer's body in the grave is *"still united to Christ"*. This is because the believer is united to Christ as a whole person, body and soul. This union can never be dissolved, so even when the believer's soul and body are separated from each other, they are never separated from Christ. Even the body of a believer is precious to Christ.

"As soon as the believer dies their soul goes to heaven."

Q Something to think about...

- Balaam expressed a wish to *"die the death of the righteous."* Why is this desirable?

Personal reflection

If someone is going to die the death of the righteous, they first have to live the life of the righteous. Do you find that the cost of this lifestyle outweighs the benefit of a good death? Or are you living with the Lord in such a way that death will only be the door into the closer presence of the Lord?

What will happen at the resurrection?

When a believer dies, their soul goes to heaven. But even arriving in glory is not the last of the blessings which Christ has purchased for His people. Question 38 explains what blessings believers will receive at the resurrection.

💬 What benefits do believers receive from Christ at the resurrection?

At the resurrection, believers being raised up in glory, shall be openly acknowledged and acquitted in the day of judgment, and made perfectly blessed in the full enjoying of God to all eternity.

There will be a resurrection

"The resurrection" refers to the time when God will raise the bodies of all those who have ever lived, and reunite them to their souls.

Everyone will have their own body resurrected. It will be the very same body, although with different properties. No matter how decayed the body is, or even if it was completely destroyed by fire, it will be raised again. God will do this by His almighty power.

> "The resurrected body of a believer will be imperishable, full of splendour, powerful, and perfectly suited to be the temple of the Holy Spirit."

Believers will be *"raised up in glory."* This is a summary of Paul's teaching that the body of a believer will be raised *"in incorruption ... in glory ... in power ... spiritual"* (1 Corinthians 15:42-44). The resurrected body of a believer will be imperishable, full of splendour, powerful, and perfectly suited to be the temple of the Holy Spirit.

Very little is said in Scripture about the resurrected body of an unbeliever. We can only imagine that it must be in dreadful contrast to a believer's body. It will not be raised in glory but in dishonour and disgrace, to *"shame and everlasting contempt"* (Daniel 12:2).

There will be a judgment

Judgment will immediately follow the resurrection. Jesus has told us what will happen. *"Then shall he sit upon the throne of his glory: and before him shall be gathered all nations: and he shall separate them one from another, as a shepherd divideth his sheep from the goats"* (Matthew 25:31-46).

In this judgment, believers will be *"openly acknowledged and acquitted."* They will be *acknowledged* - Christ will not be ashamed to name them and recognise them as His brethren and His beloved people. They will be *acquitted* - Christ will completely clear them of any guilt, on the basis of His own righteousness imputed to them, and vindicate them from all the false accusations of their enemies. Christ will acknowledge and acquit them *openly* - publicly, in front of everyone, angels and humans, good and bad.

Here is another terrible contrast with unbelievers. In the judgment, unbelievers will be publicly disowned. Christ will say to them, *"I never knew you"* (Matthew 7:23). They will be publicly condemned. Christ will cite their wicked deeds and pronounce the sentence they deserve, *"Depart from me, ye cursed, into everlasting fire"* (Matthew 25:41-46).

There will be **a reward**

For unbelievers, the outcome of the judgment is that they will go away into everlasting punishment. This is only what their sins deserve. Their own consciences will confirm that God is only being just when they receive this sentence.

For believers, it could not be more different. After the judgment believers receive yet more blessings from Christ. They are *"made perfectly blessed."* They are set entirely free from sin and sorrow. They are put fully in possession of all happiness. Each will be as blessed as it is possible for them to be. Specifically they have their blessedness *"in the full enjoying of God."* The enjoying of God is how they are made perfectly blessed.

- They will enjoy God by seeing Him, gazing on Him and feasting the eyes of their soul on Him without obstruction, distraction or interruption. *"As for me, I will behold thy face in righteousness: I shall be satisfied, when I awake, with thy likeness"* (Psalm 17:15).
- They will enjoy God by having God Himself as their eternal life and happiness. They will be with Christ, which is far better. They will rest in God, in a never-ending Sabbath. They will perfectly love, worship, and adore God, the Father, Son, and Holy Spirit, and have a full sense of the love of God for them. *"The Lamb which is in the midst of the throne shall feed them, and shall lead them unto living fountains of waters"* (Revelation 7:17).
- They will enjoy God *"to all eternity,"* for ever and ever. The Lord's redeemed ones can look forward to *"everlasting joy"* (Isaiah 51:11) with the Lord as their *"everlasting light"* (Isaiah 60:19). They will be delighted to worship the Lord endlessly, and the Lord is delighted to bless them to all eternity. *"So shall we ever be with the Lord"* (1 Thessalonians 4:17).

> "They will perfectly love, worship, and adore God, the Father, Son, and Holy Spirit, and have a full sense of the love of God for them."

⌕ Something to think about...

- Why should unbelievers be afraid of the resurrection and judgment? Why should believers not be afraid?

Personal reflection

What is your idea of perfect blessedness? Does it include enjoying God?

The story is told of a believer who sat in church with her unbelieving son. He noticed that the sermon made her very sad, and this surprised him as the sermon was about heaven. When they got home, he asked her why she was sad when she herself was going to heaven. She replied that although she would be there, she was sad because her son gave every sign of being on the way to a lost eternity. Her words were blessed to her son and made him seek the mercy of God. If you are a believer, do you long for others to have the same hope of a blessed resurrection as you do? If you are not a believer, does the prospect of judgment and eternity not give you any reason to seek the Lord while He may be found?

What does God require of us?

We come now to the second part of the Shorter Catechism. So far, up to Question 38, we have been taking a comprehensive look at what we must believe. We have covered what we should believe about God, creation, the fall, the Redeemer, and redemption. Now, from Question 39 onwards, we start to look at what we must do. In brief, we must obey God. In more detail, Questions 40-81 will spell out what shape our obedience should take.

39. What is the duty which God requireth of man?

The duty which God requireth of man, is obedience to his revealed will.

40. What did God at first reveal to man for the rule of his obedience?

The rule which God at first revealed to man for his obedience, was the moral law.

41. Where is the moral law summarily comprehended?

The moral law is summarily comprehended in the ten commandments.

Must we do what God requires?

Fallen sinners do not like being told what they must do. Since sin came into the world we have rebelled against the authority of God, wanting instead to go our own way and do our own thing. Most people like to think that God has nothing whatever to do with us or how we live our lives. Most people would say that we can live our lives as we wish, doing what makes us most happy and content, as long as we do not harm anyone. People deny that there is any God-given rule of right and wrong for our lives.

However, the fact is that God does make requirements of us. He has the right to require whatever He wishes from His own creatures. Because He is holy, He will only ever require of us what is right and holy. As His creatures, accountable to Him, we owe Him whatever He requires.

Question 39 tells us that God requires us to **"obedience."** We all have to obey God, at all times and in all situations. God requires us to obey **"his revealed will."** He does not keep His requirements a secret, so that we have to guess what might or might not please Him. He has revealed what He wants us to do.

> "People deny that there is any God-given rule of right and wrong for our lives."

How we know what God requires

Question 40 tells us that God originally revealed **_"the moral law"_** as the rule for our obedience. This law was written into human nature when we were first created. It is a statement of what is simply right and wrong, purely because of the holiness of God. At times, God has added other kinds of laws (sometimes called 'positive law'). These are things which God chooses to require, or not require, as He pleases. For example, forbidding Adam and Eve to eat the fruit of a certain tree was a 'positive law.' It was perfectly possible that God might not have required this, or required something different. But the moral law is what God requires necessarily. It is impossible for God to require anything else or anything different from the moral law.

Question 41 informs us that the moral law is **_"summarily comprehended,"_** or summarised for us, in the Ten Commandments. These were given by God on two tables of stone and delivered to Moses on Mount Sinai.

🔍 Something to think about...

- Since God has revealed how He wants us to behave, are there any legitimate excuses for disobedience? According to Romans 1:28, what is the source of our unwillingness to accept God's law?

Personal reflection

How do you respond to the fact that God has the right to make demands on us? Do you resent God's requirements for how to behave, or do you welcome God's guidance for how to live your life?

How do you sum up the Ten Commandments?

The Ten Commandments can be summarised in one word, love.

> 💬 What is the sum of the ten commandments?
>
> The sum of the ten commandments is, To love the Lord our God with all our heart, with all our soul, with all our strength, and with all our mind; and our neighbour as ourselves.

Love to **God**

The first four commandments, sometimes called the first table of the law, are concerned with our relationship to God. In Deuteronomy 6 Moses addresses Israel and says, *"Hear, O Israel: The LORD our God is one LORD: And thou shalt love the Lord thy God with all thine heart, and with all thy soul, and with all thy might"* (verses 4 & 5). These verses tell us that above all others we are to love the Lord. We are to love Him with all our vigour and strength. All our faculties are to be put to this use. Our heart, soul and mind are to unite with this one goal and purpose. Furthermore we are to love God with total sincerity, not half-heartedly or in a mere outward show. We are to love constantly and completely, without wavering in any way or to any extent. In other words, we are to love God perfectly every moment of every day. Obedience will bring a blessing but disobedience carries a terrible curse. *"Behold, I set before you this day a blessing and a curse; a blessing, if ye obey the commandments of the LORD your God, which I command you this day: and a curse, if ye will not obey the commandments of the Lord your God, but turn aside out of the way which I command you this day"* (Deuteronomy 11:26-28).

Love to **our neighbour**

The remaining six commandments, sometimes called the second table of the law, contain our duty to love our neighbour. This does not mean only the person who lives next door. All our fellow human beings are our neighbours. We are to love everyone else and seek their good as much as our own. We are to have an attitude that is totally free from selfishness, not just occasionally but all the time.

Taking the two tables of the law we are reminded of what Jesus said in the sermon on the mount, *"Be ye therefore perfect, even as your Father in heaven is perfect"* (Matthew 5:48). This is what God commands.

> "All our fellow human beings are our neighbours."

Love **all the time**

The requirements of God's law are spiritual and they extend to every thought, word and action. They embrace all of our life and apply to everyone at all times and places. We must love God with all that we are all of the time. We must also love our as ourselves all of the time. We are to be free from selfishness all of the time. None of us are like that. The Bible tells us that no one keeps God's law perfectly (Ecclesiastes 7:20). Have you discovered that in your own experience?

Q **Something to think about...**

- Is it possible to love your neighbour if you don't love God in the first instance?
- Is it possible to love God too much?
- Is it possible to love God and at the same time hate your neighbour?
- How can you tell if you really love God?
- Why is it important to devote ourselves to loving God in keeping His commandments even though we cannot keep them perfectly?

Personal reflection
What do you devote yourself to? Does the Lord God absorb all the energies of your heart, soul, strength, and mind?

Has your failure to keep God's law completely all of the time driven you in desperation to the Lord Jesus Christ as your only help?

Why should we keep the Ten Commandments?

A preface is a short introduction to a document, often by the author. God prefaced the Ten Commandments with the words, "I am the Lord thy God, which have brought thee out of the land of Egypt, out of the house of bondage." This preface is not to be skipped over quickly for it contains very significant teaching. In the preface the Lord gives reasons as to why we should keep these commandments.

💬 What is the preface to the ten commandments?

A. The preface to the ten commandments is in these words, "I am the Lord thy God, which have brought thee out of the land of Egypt, out of the house of bondage."

💬 What doth the preface to the ten commandments teach us?

A. The preface to the ten commandments teacheth us, that because God is the Lord, and our God, and Redeemer, therefore we are bound to keep all his commandments.

Because God **is the Lord**

The preface to the Ten Commandments tells us that we are obliged to keep all God's commandments because God is **"the Lord,"** Jehovah, the Most High over all the earth. We are obliged to obey Him because He is our Creator and supreme sovereign. This is the first and fundamental reason why we owe Him our obedience.

Because God **is our God**

The Lord God is a God in covenant with His people. He says, **"I am thy God."** They are in a special relationship with Him. All He is and all He has becomes ours when He makes Himself our God. Over and above the fact that He is the Lord, the fact that He is our God should give us an even stronger motivation to please Him by obeying Him. This special covenant relationship not only provides a motivation for us to obey His commandments, but it also grants the strength and ability to obey. *"This shall be the covenant that I will make with the house of Israel ... I will put my law in their inward parts, and write it in their hearts"* (Jeremiah 31:33).

"We are obliged to obey Him because He is our Creator and supreme sovereign."

Because God **is our Redeemer**

It was the Lord who took the Israelites out of Egypt and redeemed them from their bondage and slavery there. The exodus from Egypt was not the result of great planning and courage on their part. The mighty Lord had delivered them. It was a long-promised deliverance, a never to be forgotten deliverance, an unusual deliverance, and a deliverance they could never have brought about for themselves. They were now duty bound to obey Him as their Redeemer. The same applies to us if the Lord has redeemed us from spiritual slavery and bondage to sin. Surely the thought of the love of God sending His Son into the world to deliver us from sin and Satan will be a huge incentive to us to obey God as our Redeemer.

A **caution**

The preface challenges us to keep before our minds the majesty and the holiness of God and our own accountability. We are cautioned to be careful in our attitude to the commandments and to the Lord who has given them to us. The commandments are not to be broken lightly for He is the Lord God.

Someone might object and say that these things belonged to the Old Testament. They will argue that we are no longer obliged to keep the law as Israel was. But this is to misunderstand the nature of the *moral* law, as the law that the Ten Commandments summarise. It is impossible that God could cease to require us to keep the moral law. This objection also misunderstands the gospel. The Lord Jesus made very clear that He had not come to destroy the law. Without doubt, our relationship to God and His law is changed when we are converted. However, conversion does not reduce our obligation to obey God; in fact it increases our obligation. Israel were redeemed and were expected to keep the law *because* they had been saved. Having received even greater blessings in Christ, the New Testament believer is under an even greater obligation to keep God's law than their Old Testament counterpart. The Lord says to all His disciples, **"If ye love me, keep my commandments"** (John 14:15).

"If ye love me, keep my commandments. (John 14:15)"

Incidentally, there might be someone reading this who believes that in order to be saved they have to keep the Ten Commandments. Apart from the fact that none of us can ever keep the Ten Commandments, we have to grasp that such thinking is totally wrong. We are not saved because we obey God. We are saved despite the fact that we do not obey God. God's law is like a mirror reflecting to us both the perfect righteousness of God and our own sinfulness and failure to keep it. The law is meant to give us the knowledge of sin (Romans 3:20; 4:15; 5:13; 7:7-11). It does this to point to the fact that we need a Redeemer. By showing us our need of pardon and our danger of damnation the law helps to lead us in repentance and faith to Christ, the only Redeemer (Galatians 3:19-24). But those who are redeemed are then enabled to begin to obey God with a loving heart by the Holy Spirit's grace.

An **encouragement**

If the sovereign God is also our Redeemer, the preface is a source of encouragement to us to keep His commandments. Recalling what the Lord has done for us encourages us to continue to trust in Him now and into the future. It is also helpful to consider that God's purpose in redeeming sinners is so that they will be enabled to serve Him. His purpose in delivering us from spiritual bondage is that we may serve Him without fear, in holiness and righteousness all our days. We can therefore appeal to Him for help to carry out the duty of keeping all His commandments.

🔍 Something to think about...

- What are the similarities between the historical slavery in Egypt which Israel suffered, and the spiritual slavery to sin and to Satan which sinners still experience?
- What are the similarities between God delivering Israel from Egypt as a historical event, and God delivering sinners from their sins?
- If you don't know God as your own God and Redeemer, are you exempt from keeping His commandments? Can you see how the law is like a signpost? It points you to the only Redeemer from the law's condemnation of your sin.
- If you do know God as your own God and Redeemer, how does this give you extra reasons for keeping His commandments?

Whom must we worship?

The Catechism now starts to work systematically through the Ten Commandments. For each in turn, the Catechism will recite the commandment itself, then explain what we should do, then explain what we should not do.

Questions 45 and 46 begin this pattern. The first commandment teaches us who we are to worship - the only true God.

---

45 Which is the first commandment?

A. The first commandment is, "Thou shalt have no other gods before me."

---

46 What is required in the first commandment?

A. The first commandment requireth us to know and acknowledge God to be the only true God, and our God; and to worship and glorify him accordingly.

God is to be **known and acknowledged**

The first commandment requires us to *"know"* that the only true God exists. It requires us to know God as He really is, not according to how we imagine Him but as His Word reveals Him. It requires us also to know Him in Christ, as the just God and the Saviour.

The first commandment also requires us to *"acknowledge"* that God alone is the true God and that all other gods are false idols. We must do this on the personal level in our own souls as we worship God as individuals. We must also openly acknowledge God in front of other people, as appropriate and as opportunity arises. This includes making a profession of faith and sitting at the Lord's supper if we are saved. As far as we are able, we should also remind our nation and those who rule over us that they too have a duty to

> "We are to know and acknowledge God to be the only true God, and our God."

acknowledge the Lord as the only true God and to obey His commandments.

We are to know and acknowledge God to be *"the only true God, and our God"*. Knowing and acknowledging God to be the only true God saves us from atheism, but we must also come to a saving knowledge of God as our own covenant God in Christ. The first commandment therefore requires faith and repentance.

God is to be **worshipped**

Our knowledge of Jehovah as *"the only true God and our God"* is not only to fill our minds as information but this knowledge should also lead us to worship Him (Psalm 95:6). God must be the One whom we supremely adore and reverence. We should think highly of Him and speak highly of Him. We should love Him, desire Him, delight in Him, and believe Him.

"God must be the One whom we supremely adore and reverence."

Not only is He to be worshipped but this commandment makes clear that He *alone* is to be worshipped. The Israelites were not to join with others in Canaan when they worshipped their false gods. This commandment is totally contrary to the popular idea that it does not matter what your religion is or who you worship. Evidently according to this commandment it matters a great deal.

God is to be **glorified**

As the Lord is ***"the only true God and our God,"*** we are to live in a way that honours Him and brings Him glory. He is to be honoured every day and in every area of our lives, as well as in worship or religious activities. We should only ever think, speak, and act in such a way that we give all possible glory to Him and a way that makes it clear that we believe that all possible perfection belongs to Him. We must do all in our power to grow in knowledge and understanding of Him. Even when we cannot do this, we are still obliged to do it as our moral duty. Even when we cannot do this, we are still obliged to do it as our moral duty. This includes coming to choose Him, love Him, fear Him and trust Him as our Lord and Saviour, and then living accordingly.

🔍 **Something to think about...**

- What is the difference between knowing and acknowledging God as (on the one hand) the only true God and (on the other hand) as our God?
- What are some examples of worshipping and glorifying God: (a) inwardly in our souls? and (b) outwardly in our behaviour?

Why must we worship God alone?

The first commandment not only tells us what we are required to do in terms of worshipping God, it also warns us against what we should not do (Question 47). The Catechism also picks up some of the wording of the first commandment to explain what special reinforcement it gives to encourage us to obey and to dissuade us from disobedience (Question 48).

47 What is forbidden in the first commandment?

A. The first commandment forbiddeth the denying, or not worshipping and glorifying the true God, as God, and our God; and the giving of that worship and glory to any other, which is due to him alone.

48 What are we specially taught by these words, "before me" in the first commandment?

A. These words "before me" in the first commandment, teach us, That God, who seeth all things, taketh notice of, and is much displeased with, the sin of having any other god.

The exclusivity of God

The first commandment forbids *atheism*, that is, the denying of God. Some people deny that any God exists at all. Some people deny the existence of the one true God of the Bible, for example by denying the Trinity, or by saying that the idea of God is just a social construct. Some people give little thought to the philosophical question of whether God exists or not, but in practice they go about their lives from day to day as if the God of the Bible did not exist. All these forms of atheism are forbidden by the first commandment.

The first commandment also forbids *idolatry*, the worshipping and glorifying of any false god or idol. It also forbids mixing the worship of the one true God with idol worship, or worshipping the one true God along with idols. We are not to be like the people we read of in 2 Kings 17:33 who *"feared the Lord, and served their own gods."* We must not pretend, even for the sake of keeping the peace, that such activities do not matter.

The eye of God

Question 48 highlights the words *"before me"* in the first commandment. These words remind us that God sees all things. Everything happens in His presence. He sees our hearts and what we value and who we honour, as if it was all openly on display in front of Him.

God observes our keeping of all His commandments. But He takes special notice of the sin of having any other god. As the psalmist says, *"If we have forgotten the name of our*

"He sees our hearts and what we value and who we honour, as if it was all openly on display in front of Him."

God, or stretched out our hands to a strange god, shall not God search this out? For he knoweth the secrets of the heart" (Psalm 44:20-21).

God is greatly displeased with the sin of having any other God. It is a great evil. He will not tolerate any rivals. If we entertain any competitor we are insulting God to His face. *"I am the Lord: that is my name: and my glory I will not give to another"* (Isaiah 42:8). Belshazzar forgot this and his punishment swiftly followed. Although our punishment may not be so dramatic, we need not think that it will be any less if we bring God's displeasure on ourselves by breaking this commandment.

🔍 Something to think about...

Personal reflection

People can be atheists in practice even if they do not label themselves as atheists. On a day to day basis, do you more or less forget about God, or do you actively acknowledge and worship God in every aspect of your life?

Even people who know about the one living and true God can be guilty of the sin of having some other God. Paul mentions the tragic and desperate case of those whose god is their belly, and whose mind is set on earthly things (Philippians 3.19). When God looks at your heart, does He see any inferior gods taking His place in your life, or does He see loyalty to Him alone?

How are we to worship?

After the first commandment has shown us who we are to worship, we come now to the second commandment, which directs us how we are to worship. Instead of worshipping God by means that we invent for ourselves as we think best, we are to worship Him by means of the ordinances which He has appointed.

49 Which is the second commandment?

A. The second commandment is, "Thou shalt not make unto thee any graven image, or any likeness of any thing that is in heaven above, or that is in the earth beneath, or that is in the water under the earth: Thou shalt not bow down thyself to them, nor serve them: for I the Lord thy God am a jealous God, visiting the iniquity of the fathers upon the children, unto the third and fourth generation of them that hate me; and showing mercy unto thousands of them that love me, and keep my commandments."

50 What is required in the second commandment?

A. The second commandment requireth the receiving, observing, and keeping pure and entire, all such religious worship and ordinances as God hath appointed in his Word.

We have received instructions

The Lord is not only emphatic that He, and He alone, is the object of our worship, He is also very categorical as to how we worship Him. In His Word He has given us rules for our guidance. This was true in the Old Testament and it is also true in the New Testament. When the Lord sent out His apostles with the gospel they were told to go to the nations, *"teaching them to observe all things whatsoever I have commanded you"* (Matthew 28:20), including His instructions regarding the nature and content of worship. It is not only our duty to worship God but to do so only as He Himself commands.

"It is not only our duty to worship God but to do so only as He Himself commands."

The *"religious worship and ordinances as God hath appointed in His Word"* primarily include prayer and praise in the name of Christ, the reading, preaching, and hearing of the Word, and the administration of the sacraments. They also include ordinances such as church government and discipline, and the gospel ministry, as well as more personal, occasional ordinances such as fasting and vowing to the Lord.

Down through the years many people have wrongly said that it doesn't really matter exactly how you worship God. As long as you are sincere the outward details are not all that important. This commandment corrects this view by making clear to us that the outward details, as well as the inward condition of our hearts, are of great importance.

We must follow these instructions

Question 50 tells us that the *"receiving and observing"* of the instructions of the Lord are to be *"pure and entire."*

- We have to *receive* the form of worship which God has appointed in His Word, accepting that it has God's authority and acknowledging its binding obligation on us.
- We have to *observe* the form of worship which God has appointed, putting it into practice in our lives by actually participating in prayer, praise, reading and hearing the Word preached, and so on.
- We have to receive and accept God's appointed worship in a *pure* form. Once we know from the Word of God what God requires, we must keep it free from our own additions and whatever things we imagine will improve it.
- We have to receive and accept God's appointed worship *in its entirety.* We should not miss out any of God's ordinances, or any part of the ordinances, at the appropriate times for observing them.

> "It is the Bible which regulates or governs the way we worship."

At the time of the Reformation in Europe the men of God who led the church were mindful of this commandment. They were concerned that the people would be freed from all the superstition and idolatry of mediaeval times, and carefully instructed in how the Lord wanted them to worship Him. This was particularly true in Scotland, where great care was taken to receive and observe all the guidelines for the worship of God. To this day our worship is governed by the instructions we find in our Bibles. It is the Bible which regulates or governs the way we worship. In this way we try to obey what the Lord commanded in Deuteronomy, *"What thing soever I command you, observe to do it: thou shalt not add thereto, nor diminish from it"* (12:32). For instance, we use only psalms in worship, because this is what the Lord gave the Book of Psalms to the church to be used for. Nor do we use musical instruments in worship, because the Lord has not ordained instruments to be used at any point in New Testament worship.

🔍 Something to think about...

- The wording of the second commandment shows that there are ways of attempting to worship God which displease God very displeased. How can we know if our attempts to worship God will be acceptable to Him?
- Think of some ordinances of worship and classify them according to whether they are personal, individual acts of worship or corporate, acts of worship. In what ways are you (or are you not) keeping them *'pure and entire'* according to the Word of God?

Can we amend God's way of worship?

Now that we have seen what the second commandment requires, we are moving on to look at what it forbids (Question 51) and the reasons it provides to encourage us to keep it (Question 52).

51. What is forbidden in the second commandment?

A. The second commandment forbiddeth the worshipping of God by images, or any other way not appointed in his Word.

52. What are the reasons annexed to the second commandment?

A. The reasons annexed to the second commandment are, God's sovereignty over us, his propriety in us, and the zeal he hath to his own worship.

Two clear errors

(a) Idolatry

The second commandment explicitly forbids making images to worship.

It also prohibits us from attempting to worship God by images of any creature (whether animal, human, spirit, or angel), or using images of creatures in the worship of God.

"Adding to what God has specified may mean that our worship pleases us, but it will certainly not please God."

The second commandment also forbids any sort of image of the true God. This applies whether the image is glass, paper or stone, or an actor impersonating a divine being. Obviously it also applies to every person of the Godhead, including the Lord Jesus Christ. This is why we should not have pictures of Jesus in our churches or in our homes and why we should avoid books which contain such pictures.

(b) Imagination

The second commandment teaches us that we are not to use our own imaginations and do what we like in worship. We are to include in our worship only what God has specifically instructed. Adding to what God has specified may mean that our worship pleases us, but it will certainly not please God. People justify all sorts of worship practices in all sorts of ways — either because it's traditional or because it's contemporary, either to make it look better or sound more beautiful, either to be more inclusive or to showcase special talent. In reality, the only thing that needs to concern us is whether God has commanded it in His Word.

Three good reasons

Three reasons are attached to the second commandment why we should carefully observe it.

> "He has the perfect right to regulate the way in which we worship Him."

(a) God is sovereign over us
As King of kings and Lord of lords He has the perfect right to regulate the way in which we worship Him. *"O come, let us worship and bow down: let us kneel before the Lord our maker"* (Psalm 95:6-7).

(b) God has propriety in us
God views us as belonging to Him, as His possession. We belong to Him not just because He has made us, but because He has redeemed us. *"I have redeemed thee, I have called thee by thy name; thou art mine"* (Isaiah 43:1). This relationship is an additional incentive to worship God only in the way that pleases Him.

(c) God is jealous for his own worship
Obviously God is not jealous in the sinful way that we get jealous. This is a way of saying that He carefully guards His own worship from corruption and error. God sees His relationship with His people as something so precious that protects His honour when anything spoils it, especially when it takes to do with something so special as the manner in which they worship Him.

God shows his zeal for his own worship in two ways:

- **When people break the second commandment,** God interprets this as hating Him. Once one generation becomes ungodly, as parents they go on to teach their children to be idolaters. When the children follow the example of their parents and go on to show their own hatred for God by also breaking this commandment, then the subsequent generations, like the parents, feel the judgment of God.
- **When people keep the second commandment,** God sees this as loving Him. Parents who teach their children to avoid idolatry are a great blessing. Such parents and children will know the blessing of the Lord, even for thousands of generations.

🔍 Something to think about...

- When discussing what we do in worship services, people sometimes say that if God has not forbidden something, it must be legitimate for us to include it in worship. How does the second commandment contradict this view?
- While God's vengeance extends to three or four generations, His mercy extends to thousands of generations. How does this help to shape your response to the requirements of the second commandment?

What attitude do we need to worship God?

Now that we have seen who we are to worship and the means of worshipping Him, the third commandment tells us about our attitude towards God and His worship. We should worship God with the deepest respect and reverence.

In our society this is regarded as a very unimportant matter. People are very concerned about our behaviour towards one another, and towards creation and animals, but very unconcerned about our conduct towards God. We do not have the fear, awe and respect for God which this commandment requires. When names such as God or Jesus are used as a curse, generally people do not regard this as much of a sin. But as the psalmist reminds us, "holy and reverend is his name" (Psalm 111:9), and in this commandment God clearly requires us to treat His name with the utmost reverence. Even the things of God must be treated with great reverence.

---

53 Which is the third commandment?

A. The third commandment is, "Thou shalt not take the name of the Lord thy God in vain: for the Lord will not hold him guiltless that taketh His name in vain."

54 What is required in the third commandment?

A. The third commandment requireth the holy and reverent use of God's names, titles, attributes, ordinances, Word and works.

How do we reverence God's name?

The requirement to use God's name in a holy and reverent way is not just restricted to using the actual names God or Jesus. This question reminds us that *"the name of ... God"* refers to anything by which He makes Himself known to us. Question 54 highlights various ways in which God makes Himself known to us.

> "We should worship God with the deepest respect and reverence."

(a) His names, titles, attributes

God has given Himself *"names"* which are intended to tell us something about who He is and what He is like. His names include Lord (sovereign ruler), Jehovah (a God in covenant with His people to redeem them) and I AM (the self-existent, absolute God).

The Bible also tells us some of God's *titles*, which reveal how He interacts with others, both as His creatures and as His redeemed people. His titles include the King of Kings and the Father of mercies.

Scripture also reveals something about God's *"attributes,"* including His holiness, justice, mercy, wisdom and unchangeableness. Paul speaks of God as *"eternal, immortal, invisible, the only wise God"* (1 Timothy 1:17).

We show our reverence to God's names, titles, and attributes when we are impressed with the sight they give us of the majesty and glory of God, and when we fill our minds with humble and adoring thoughts of Him, and when we only ever speak of Him in a sober and respectful way.

(b) His **ordinances**

God also makes Himself known through His ordinances. These include prayer, hearing the Bible preached, the sacraments of baptism and the Lord's supper, and praise. We show our reverence to God's ordinances by attending worship diligently and participating in it sincerely, with a view to honouring Him. When we gather for worship or read our Bibles we are to remember that we are engaging in holy things and not to think of them as being like any other activity we take part in (Ecclesiastes 5:1).

(c) His **Word**

The Word of God here refers to the Scriptures of the Old and New Testament. We use the Word in a holy and reverent way by hearing the voice of God speaking with authority in it, taking its message home to our own hearts, and lovingly putting it into practice in our lives.

> "We use redemption to God's honour when we comply with His scheme of salvation."

(d) His **works**

The works of God include creation, providence, and redemption.

We use *creation* to God's honour when we thank Him for what He has made and when we use His gifts in creation to help us become more devoted to Him.

We use *providence* to God's honour when we are satisfied with how He is managing everything, when we praise Him for the mercies He gives us, and when we trustingly bear the afflictions He sends us.

We use *redemption* to God's honour when we comply with His scheme of salvation — accepting His verdict on our sinfulness, recognising that Christ crucified is the power and the wisdom of God, and receiving and resting on Christ alone for our salvation.

Oaths and vows

The third commandment also applies to oaths and vows. To give an oath or vow is very solemn because it calls God to witness that we will keep our word. In fact, it is an act of worship. By swearing an oath or vow we acknowledge that God is able to discern whether we are sincere in what we promise and that He is certain to punish us if we break our word. The difference between oaths and vows is that oaths are normally made between one person and another (calling God to witness), while vows are made directly to God and relate directly to religious matters to do with the glory of God and the salvation of our souls.

Of course, we are obliged to keep our promises whether or not we take an oath about them. But adding an oath is an extra, solemn step for exceptionally important matters. We should only take an oath about our commitment to fulfil a promise when the business is very serious (for example, when a man and a woman get married they promise to be faithful to each other for life). Similarly we should only take an oath about the truthfulness of what we say if the subject matter is very weighty (for example, if we give evidence under oath in a court of law, where a judge is determining whether someone has committed a crime).

"By swearing an oath or vow we acknowledge that God is able to discern whether we are sincere in what we promise and that He is certain to punish us if we break our word."

🔍 Something to think about...

- Draw up a list of several names and titles given to God in the Bible. What information does each give us about God, and how should we put that specific information to use when we worship Him?

Personal reflection

The song they sing in heaven includes a rhetorical question. *"Great and marvellous are thy works, Lord God Almighty; just and true are thy ways, thou King of saints. Who shall not fear thee, O Lord, and glorify thy name? For thou only art holy"* (Revelation 15:3-4). Do you fear the Lord and glorify His name?

How do we **show respect for God?**

If the third commandment requires a reverent use of God's name, Question 55 tells us that it forbids a profane use of God's name. The reason added to the commandment is given in Question 56.

55 What is forbidden in the third commandment?

A. The third commandment forbiddeth all profaning or abusing of anything whereby God maketh himself known.

56 What is the reason annexed to the third commandment?

A. The reason annexed to the third commandment is, That however the breakers of this commandment may escape punishment from men, yet the Lord our God will not suffer them to escape his righteous judgment.

Profanity **prohibited**

The third commandment forbids us using irreverently or wrongly any of the things which God makes Himself known by. Everything connected with God is holy and sacred.

Yet it is common to hear God's names being taken in vain, and used lightly and thoughtlessly as a curse. Also when things go wrong in our lives or when some terrible tragedy occurs people will often blame God, casting doubt on His goodness, wisdom and holiness. To think and talk in this way is to take God's name in vain.

We can also take God's name in vain by sneering and mocking at the doctrines of His Word, or at the life of godliness, or at Christians who are trying to live to God's glory in obedience to His Word. Similarly, if we call ourselves Christians, and then live in a way which brings dishonour and reproach on the name of God or Christ, then again we are profaning and abusing something

"Everything connected with God is holy and sacred."

which God uses as a way of making Himself known in the world.

But there are many other ways in which we become guilty of taking God's name in vain. If we just speak of Him without thought or awe, we are guilty. If we fail to attend worship when we should, we are guilty of breaking this commandment. If, when we do attend worship, we while away the time by sleeping or daydreaming about other things, then we are taking the Lord's name in vain.

Isaiah pointed out that Israel broke this commandment by offering worship which was not wholehearted. The Lord refused to accept their worship and declared His unhappiness with it. *"Bring no more vain oblations; incense is an abomination unto me; the new moons and sabbaths, the calling of assemblies, I cannot away with; it is iniquity, even the solemn meeting. Your new moons and your appointed feasts my soul hateth; they are a trouble unto me; I am weary to bear them"* (Isaiah 1:13-14). We have the same warning in the New Testament where Christ says, *"Woe unto you, scribes and Pharisees, hypocrites! . . . for a pretence (ye) make long prayer: therefore ye shall receive the greater damnation"* (Matthew 23:14).

Profanity **punished**

Typically people are not very concerned about the issue of treating God's names with respect. Most people would laugh at the thought of punishing anyone for taking God's name in vain. They certainly don't react to blasphemy in a way that makes the blasphemer feel they've done anything wrong.

> "Profanity is completely inappropriate on our part and highly offensive to Him."

However, Question 56 points out that God doesn't treat our disrespect as an insignificant thing. He is *"the Lord,"* who deserves our utmost reverence, and He is *"our God,"* who we owe so much to in both providence and grace. Profanity is completely inappropriate on our part and highly offensive to Him. He will therefore most certainly and most righteously punish everyone who is guilty of breaking this commandment, if not in this life, in eternity.

God's justice will certainly be carried out against them (Zechariah 5:3). Just as it is certain that there will be a judgment seat, before which sinners must appear, it is certain that this sin will be judged and punished (Malachi 3:5). They may escape punishment from men but they cannot escape from God as judge.

Q **Something to think about...**

- How do you take God's name in vain if you question and doubt God's Word, or if you go through the motions of worshipping Him without being wholehearted about it?
- What is the harm in taking God's name in vain?

When does God especially want to be worshipped?

So far, we have looked at commandments which tell us (1) who we are to worship, (2) the means of worshipping Him, and (3) our attitude as we worship Him. Now we come to (4) the times when we are to worship Him. We are to worship Him at whatever set times He has appointed in His Word, and specifically, one whole day in every seven.

57 Which is the fourth commandment?

A. The fourth commandment is, "Remember the sabbath Day, to keep it holy. Six days shalt thou labour, and do all thy work; but the seventh day is the Sabbath of the Lord thy God: in it thou shalt not do any work, thou, nor thy son, nor thy daughter, thy man-servant, nor thy maid-servant, nor thy cattle, nor thy stranger that is within thy gates: for in six days the Lord made heaven and earth, the sea, and all that in them is, and rested the seventh day: wherefore the Lord blessed the Sabbath-day, and hallowed it."

58 What is required in the fourth commandment?

A. The fourth commandment requireth the keeping holy to God such set times as he hath appointed in His Word; expressly one whole day in seven, to be a holy Sabbath to Himself.

59 Which day of the seven hath God appointed to be the weekly Sabbath?

A. From the beginning of the world to the resurrection of Christ, God appointed the seventh day of the week to be the weekly Sabbath; and the first day of the week ever since, to continue to the end of the world, which is the Christian Sabbath.

60 How is the Sabbath to be sanctified?

A. The Sabbath is to be sanctified by a holy resting all that day, even from such worldly employments and recreations as are lawful on other days; and spending the whole time in the public and private exercises of God's worship, except so much as is to be taken up in the works of necessity and mercy.

A day of **rest**

When God had finished His work of creation He left us an example of how we are to structure our week. We read in Genesis that God rested for one day, taking delight in the very good work which He had completed. He has also appointed one day in every week to be a day of rest for His creatures. We are to spend the Lord's day in *"holy resting,"* finding delight in the very good works which God has done – not only in creation, but also in grace.

It is a great kindness on the Lord's part to grant His creatures a day of rest from their ordinary weekly occupations. Since the fall, we get tired and weary and need time to rest, otherwise we will become ill and our work and lives will suffer. We also have to ensure that if we employ other people to work for us, they also get a day of rest. Even animals are allowed one day a week without work. Of course, some things are necessary to be done and some things come into the category of acts of mercy. We don't take a rest from getting dressed in the morning or eating food, and we have to continue to care for people in need. But whatever works of necessity and mercy we do, it is to be with a view to enabling the Lord's day to be kept focused on Him and His worship.

In the Old Testament this day of rest was the seventh day of the week, commemorating the completed work of creation. Following the resurrection of the Lord Jesus Christ the Christian Sabbath is held on the first day of the week, the day on which He rose from the grave, to commemorate not only creation but the completed work of redemption (Revelation. 1:10; Acts 20:7; John 20:19, 26).

"It is a great kindness on the Lord's part to grant His creatures a day of rest from their ordinary weekly occupations."

A day of **work**

At the same time as the Sabbath is a day of rest, it is also a day of work. This is not a contradiction, because the purpose of resting from our normal weekly work is to free us up to be very busy in a different kind of work – the work of worship. We are not to waste away the Sabbath day in idleness. The Sabbath is a day for worship and spiritual activity. It is a day when our souls rather than our bodies are especially busy and when the needs of our souls rather than our bodies receive our special attention. The Sabbath is a day during which we are to be especially engaged in doing business with heaven and preparing for eternity. We should be active in worship all day long, whether in the public, formal assemblies of God's people or in private, at home by ourselves or with our families. We should not rest content with giving just one little corner of the day to worship - it is meant to be a whole day of spiritual activity.

"We are not to waste away the Sabbath day in idleness. The Sabbath is a day for worship and spiritual activity."

A day **apart**

The Sabbath is a day set apart from all the others by the Lord when He claimed it for His own, and blessed it (see Genesis 2:3). Amongst other things this means that the Lord reserves the right to choose when He wants us to approach Him in worship, and He blesses those who remember His day.

He has given precious promises about being present by His Spirit when people gather in church.

The Sabbath day is set apart by us from every other day, as the one special occasion during our week when we remember the Lord our Maker and Redeemer. Our focus on this day is to be the Lord. Instead of focusing on earning our living, or ordinary pastimes, we can devote ourselves to rejoicing in God and finding our satisfaction in Him.

Specifically, we can do this when we assemble with other believers to worship God as His church –

- By hearing God's Word preached
- By joining in public prayers and praises
- By partaking of the sacraments

We can also do this when we are in private, on our own or in our families –

- By singing, praying and reading the Word on our own or as a family
- By catechising each other as a family or examining ourselves on our own
- By discussing the sermon and other spiritual topics with our families and friends
- By meditating on the truth of God's Word
- By reading edifying books

> "The Sabbath day is set apart by us from every other day, as the one special occasion during our week when we remember the Lord our Maker and Redeemer."

We also set the Sabbath day apart by remembering it.

A day remembered

For one thing, we should remember that God has kept one day special for Himself from the beginning of time, even before He called Israel to be His people, and redeemed them out of Egypt. We are therefore only following in a long line of obedient worshippers of God when we keep His day holy. For another thing, we should spend our whole week both remembering that the Sabbath has passed (for example, trying to keep in mind whatever truth we heard preached last Sabbath) and also remembering that the Sabbath is coming up again. We should make arrangements throughout the week to make sure that things won't be left unfinished to distract us from spiritual things on the Lord's day, and especially towards the end of each week we should pray for help to spend the whole day in worshipping God and for a blessing when we do so. We ought to love our neighbour by helping others to remember the sabbath to keep it holy. We should help those for whom we have responsibility to keep it. We should help them to keep the sabbath holy. We can also remember and show kindness those who cannot get out to church due to ill health and old age.

A day ahead

The Sabbath rest which we enjoy in this world is a foretaste of the rest which God's people will enjoy in heaven. Heaven is one unending Sabbath rest (see Hebrews 4:9). Worship goes on continually in heaven, without interruption, without weariness, and without conclusion. It is the place where our souls and bodies will be completely at rest in God, and where we will join harmoniously with all of God's people at once in praising and blessing Him. Our entire focus will be on adoring God for what He has done in creation and salvation.

> "Worship goes on continually in heaven, without interruption, without weariness, and without conclusion."

Q Something to think about...

- Why do we need a day of rest?
- While the Old Testament Sabbath commemorated creation, the New Testament Sabbath commemorates redemption. In what ways is redemption a greater work than creation?
- What are the similarities and differences between Sabbath on earth and the Sabbath rest in heaven?

Personal reflection
Do you enjoy the Lord's day when it comes? Do you look forward to resting from ordinary activities and being busy in spiritual activities?

How should we keep God's special day?

When God calls us to remember the Sabbath day to keep it holy, what does He forbid? Question 61 answers this. Then Question 62 looks at the reasons added to the fourth commandment to help us keep it.

💬 What is forbidden in the fourth commandment?

A. The fourth commandment forbiddeth the omission or careless performance of the duties required, and the profaning the day by idleness, or doing that which is in itself sinful, or by unnecessary thoughts, words, or works, about our worldly employments or recreations.

💬 What are the reasons annexed to the fourth commandment?

A. The reasons annexed to the fourth commandment are, God's allowing us six days of the week for our own employments, his challenging a special propriety in the seventh, his own example, and his blessing the Sabbath-day.

Idle, sinful or unnecessary

On the Lord's day, we are forbidden to do various things. We must not omit the duties of the day (as set out in Questions 58-60), or perform those duties carelessly.

Additionally, Question 61 points out that there are various things we must avoid so as not to be guilty of *"profaning"* the day,

> "God has given us six days in the week to attend to all our other concerns."

reducing it to something common and unholy. *"Idleness"* is one way of profaning the Lord's day. Another way is by doing things which would be *"sinful"* any day of the week. Sinful things become even more sinful in fact when we do them on the Lord's day. Another way is by spending *"unnecessary"* time on ordinary work or pleasure, whether in our thoughts, conversation, or activities.

Our own interests

Question 62 highlights the various reasons added to the commandment. For one thing, God is *"allowing us six days of the week for our own employments,"* whether work or leisure. God has given us six days in the week to attend to all our other concerns. He could have required us to give more time to Him — every other day, for example, or one day in three — but He gives us of plenty time every week to do all that we want and need to do in the way of looking after our own interests.

God's own **day**

God challenges *"a special propriety"* in this day. That means that He claims it as His own special possession. He gives us all our days, but He specially marks this one out as *the Lord's day.* People sometimes resent the requirement to keep the Sabbath day holy because it restricts the liberty they have to do things which are perfectly lawful on the other days of the week (earning a wage, buying and selling, sports and current affairs, etc.) But God has the right to claim our time for Himself, and it is not unreasonable for us to give our sovereign Creator what He asks for, far less our sovereign Redeemer.

God's own **example**

After God had taken six days to create the world and all it contains, He rested on the seventh day. This was not because He was tired, but to set out the pattern of activity followed by the ceasing from activity. We are to follow His example, not in the sense of trying to be superhumans who don't get tired by our work, but in the sense of taking pleasure and finding satisfaction in God's good works.

> "He blesses those who keep this day."

God's own **blessing**

God blessed this day in the sense that He has consecrated it, or set it apart for a holy use. He also blesses this day to those who keep it. He arranges His providence so that they don't lose out in their ordinary affairs when they put their ordinary business to one side for His day. And He blesses those who keep this day. He makes it a time of special blessing to them as they devote themselves to Him and His worship.

🔍 Something to think about...

Personal reflection
Review what you have done the last few weekends. Which of your habits help you to keep the Lord's day holy? Which of your habits do you need to change so that you avoid reducing the Lord's day to something unholy and profane?

Which of the reasons for keeping the fourth commandment would you use first in seeking to persuade others? How will you use this reason to help you keep the Lord's day holy this coming week?

How can we have prosperous communities?

The first four commandments make up the first table of the law – directing us how we are to love God. We move on now to look at the next six commandments, the second table of the law – directing us how we are to love our neighbour.

63 Which is the fifth commandment?

A. The fifth commandment is, "Honour thy father and thy mother; that thy days may be long upon the land which the Lord thy God giveth thee."

64 What is required in the fifth commandment?

A. The fifth commandment requireth the preserving the honour, and performing the duties, belonging to every one in their several places and relations, as superiors, inferiors, or equals.

65 What is forbidden in the fifth commandment?

A. The fifth commandment forbiddeth the neglecting of, or doing anything against, the honour and duty which belongeth to every one in their several places and relations.

66 What is the reason annexed to the fifth commandment?

A. The reason annexed to the fifth commandment is a promise of long life and prosperity (as far as it shall serve for God's glory and their own good) to all such as keep this commandment.

An obvious meaning

Our father and mother

The fifth commandment tells us that God wants us to show respect to those in authority. In the first instance, children are to honour and respect their parents. We are to speak respectfully to our parents and also about them. We are also to obey them, as long as they don't want us to disobey God. We should do nothing sinful that will cause our parents disappointment, sorrow or shame. We have an example of this in the Lord Jesus who always respected and obeyed Mary and Joseph (Luke 2:51). If parents are spared into old age, it is also the duty of children to do all they can to care for them. Again the Lord left us an example in this when He showed His concern and care for His mother even when He was on the cross (John 19:25-27).

All our seniors

As well as owing honour to our parents, we are also required to respect all our *"superiors,"* that is, anyone who is senior to us in age or gifts, or anyone in a position of authority in the family, the church, or civil society. We should think of any man or woman who is older than us as in a sense our father or our mother, and the same for anyone who has more skills or expertise in any area of life. Similarly, there are roles in the family (grandparents, uncles and aunts) and the church (ministers, elders, and deacons) and civil society (teachers, employers, magistrates, members of parliament) which grant the post-holders authority over others. We must treat these people as our seniors and respect their authority.

What does this look like in practice? Here are a few examples.

"We should do nothing sinful that will cause our parents disappointment, sorrow or shame."

(a) Teachers

Students who are rude and disobedient to their teachers, and disruptive in the classroom break the fifth commandment.

(b) Rulers

The forces of law and order in our society include the government, the courts and the police. They have a duty to stop and punish what is wicked and to help and encourage all that is good. We are to obey these rulers as long as they do not ask us to do wrong (see Acts 5:29). Even if we don't think they have the gravitas or personal characteristics to make them suitable for high office, we have to obey them out of respect for their authority. And even if they make rules which we think are pointless or unfair, whether about paying taxes or driving at certain speeds, we are to obey them (see Romans 13:1). As the Lord said, we are to *"render therefore unto Caesar the things which are Caesar's"* (Matthew 22:21).

(c) Employers

Our boss in the workplace is to be obeyed, and is not to be cheated or treated disrespectfully (Ephesians 6:5).

(d) Ministers

When the church of God ordains men to the office of minister, we should esteem them very highly in love for their work's sake, and diligently attend on their ministry. This includes making sure that we support them financially, and also that we help them as much as we can to enable them to concentrate on the Word and prayer, without the distraction of worrying about their temporal situation. We fail to keep the fifth commandment if we forget to pray for them, or spread unfair rumours about them, or disregard what they bring to us from God's Word.

Whoever our seniors are, we can honour them by:

* praying for them and thanking God for them,
* following their example when they do what is right,
* willingly doing what they tell us and taking their advice, as long as it doesn't involve disobeying God,
* accepting their correction,
* being loyal to them and not undermining them,
* putting up with their faults, and not making them out to be worse than they are,
* not resenting the fact that they have a position of authority which we don't,
* not treating them (or talking about them) with mockery, ridicule, or sarcasm.

A less obvious meaning

According to Question 64, the fifth commandment not only applies to children's behaviour towards their parents, but also to everyone in all their various and distinct relationships, whether they are in authority, under authority, or share equal status.

For example, the fifth commandment also applies to parents. Parents are required to love and care for their children. They are to teach them what is right and wrong, and give them a good example, disciplining them as the Bible instructs. Anyone who is younger than us, or less skilled than us, is in that sense our *"inferior,"* or junior. But whatever seniority we have, we have to respect our juniors. With authority comes responsibility, and the greater the authority, the greater the responsibility.

> "Parents are required to love and care for their children."

How then should we treat those who are in any sense our juniors?

- Remembering that our position of seniority is intended for their welfare, not for our glorification;
- Loving them, praying for them, and blessing them;
- Encouraging them when they do well and discouraging them from doing wrong or doing tasks badly;
- Doing what we can to help them, and not exploiting them or using our position for selfish gain;
- Not making unreasonable demands, or treating them harshly when they don't do what they've been asked to do.

Our *"equals"* are those who have the same status as us. For example, our siblings are our equals under the authority of our parents, even though some siblings are older or younger than the others. Other members of our congregation are our equals under the authority of the kirk session, even though one of them might be our boss at work and another is the mayor.

Equals should honour each other by:

- Loving one another, thinking kindly of one another *"with brotherly love, in honour preferring one another"* (Romans 12.10);
- Valuing each other's dignity and gifts, not bullying each other or being envious when someone gets on well (e.g., when someone gets better exam results, or lands a better paying job, or gets promoted more quickly);
- Provoking each other *"unto love and to good works"* (Hebrews 10.24) not enticing each other to sin.

Long life and prosperity

Going along with this commandment is *"a promise of long life and prosperity."* Those who disobey this commandment will not have the blessing of God on their lives. Those who obey this commandment will experience God's blessing.

This is true for society in general, as any society where the fifth commandment is observed is putting the conditions in place where you would naturally expect that lifespans will be lengthened and material prosperity will increase. Where there is more anarchy and unrest in society, this tends towards conditions which shorten life and decrease prosperity.

However, it is not always the case that every individual who keeps the fifth commandment will have a long and prosperous life. This promise needs to be taken with a limitation — it will be fulfilled as long as this is consistent with *"God's glory and their own good."* It might be better for somebody to be taken out of this world sooner rather than later even though they scrupulously obeyed their parents. A long and happy life in this world is desirable in itself, but it is always less valuable than endless blessedness in the world to come.

🔍 Something to think about...

- Make a list of all the people you have contact with on an average day (e.g.,family members, bus driver, colleagues or classmates, shop assistant, etc.). For each of them, identify whether you are their superior, inferior, or equal. What specific duties do you owe to each of them in this relation?

How do we show that life is precious?

Life is so precious because we are made in the image of God. It is only God who can give life, and once a person's life ends in this world, we can do nothing to bring them back. The sixth commandment requires us to preserve life and forbids us to take away life unjustly.

67 Which is the sixth commandment?

A. The sixth commandment is, Thou shalt not kill.

68 What is required in the sixth commandment?

A. The sixth commandment requireth all lawful endeavours to preserve our own life, and the life of others.

69 What is forbidden in the sixth commandment?

A. The sixth commandment forbiddeth the taking away of our own life, or the life of our neighbour unjustly, or whatsoever tendeth thereunto.

Taking care of ourselves

The sixth commandment forbids us to take away our own life, and instructs us to do all that we lawfully can to preserve and keep our life.

(a) Looking after our bodies

For one thing, we have to eat properly in order to keep our bodies healthy, neither deliberately starving ourselves nor overindulging in food. We should also keep a healthy balance between work, leisure, and sleep. Although laziness is a sin, it is also wrong to be a workaholic, for example. Also, if we are injured in an accident, or if we have a medical condition, we need to accept the appropriate therapies and medicines to reduce pain and get better.

"We should also keep a healthy balance between work, leisure, and sleep."

This commandment also means that we are not to do anything that might harm our bodies, such as smoking, excessive drinking, or substance misuse. We should also avoid taking part in activities which inherently involve foolish risks, such as violent sports, dangerous sports and unnecessary stunts.

We are also permitted, and in fact required, to use self-defence when necessary. If you are mugged in the street, or if someone breaks into your house, or if your country is invaded by an attacking army, you have the right to fight back, proportionately, to preserve your own life.

(b) Looking after our souls

As surely as we have a body to care for, each one of us also has a soul. We injure our souls every time we sin, and we endanger the life of our souls every time we resist God in unbelief. This commandment requires us to seek the salvation of our soul. The endeavours we have to use to save our souls include searching the Scriptures to find eternal life, and embracing Christ Jesus to be our own resurrection and life (John 11.25). Unless we have our sins forgiven and have been converted we will go to a lost eternity. We will be guilty of taking away the life of our own soul.

Taking care of others

As we are not free to take away our own life neither are we free to take away unjustly the lives of others, or do anything that has the tendency towards this. Parents should look after their children, doing all they can to allow them to grow up healthy and keep them from harm (for example, stopping them from playing with sharp knives or running into the road). We should do whatever we can to make sure people get the food, clothing, and housing they need. If we have employees, we should arrange that they only work reasonable hours and have sufficient leisure time. We should support scientific research into new medicines to help reduce suffering and disease; as well as support the development of new technologies to help make life easier for people with disabilities, and new agricultural methods to increase the efficiency of food production.

> "We should do whatever we can to make sure people get the food, clothing, and housing they need."

This commandment also applies to governments. The government is to do all it can to ensure that the people of the country are preserved from danger and injury. The government is primarily responsible for keeping us safe from military threats from other countries, and maintaining law and order within our country. There are also circumstances where it is appropriate for the government to take steps to reduce road traffic accidents, promote public health, ensure that buildings are constructed safely, and so on.

Let's look at some further practical examples of how to keep the sixth commandment:

(a) Vulnerable

We have a duty of care towards the vulnerable in society, including little children, unborn children, people with disabilities, people with terminal illnesses, and those who are in poor health due to extreme old age. It is a sin against the sixth commandment to treat the vulnerable as if their lives were not worthy of preservation. Being weak or ill is not a reason to deprive someone of life. In fact, their very vulnerability is itself a reason for us to put all the more effort into making their lives as comfortable and worth living as possible.

(b) Temptation

If we encourage our friends in bad habits such as drinking or taking drugs, we are guilty of breaking this commandment.

(c) Carelessness

If we cause an accident through our carelessness (for example, by driving a car without paying attention to the road, or neglecting to warn passers by about a manhole we uncovered while doing repair work), then we have broken this commandment because we have not made the basic endeavours to preserve the life of our neighbours.

(d) War

Although it breaks the sixth commandment when a country goes to war for spurious reasons or mere material self-interest, there is such a thing as a just war, which is consistent with the sixth commandment, when a nation has to defend itself from hostile forces.

> "It is a sin against the sixth commandment to treat the vulnerable as if their lives were not worthy of preservation."

(e) Execution

According to the sixth commandment, it is right for murderers to be put to death by the civil authorities as a fitting punishment for the crime of murder (see Genesis 9:6 and Romans 13:4). When a murderer is instead released from prison, and especially if they commit another murder, the government is guilty before God of breaking the sixth commandment because they failed to deal properly with the murderer in the first place.

(f) Preaching

If I saw that you were in great physical danger I would be guilty if I did not warn you. The Bible tells us we are in great spiritual danger as sinners. Preachers are commissioned by God to warn people of this and to show them how to save their life (by faith in Christ). Preachers who faithfully preach this message are keeping this commandment. If they fail to preach this, they are responsible for people losing their souls. But if people hear the faithful preaching and then ignore the warning, they themselves are guilty of breaking it by neglecting to obtain spiritual life for their souls.

Laws and tendencies

According to **Question 68**, the sixth commandment requires *"all lawful endeavours"* to preserve life.

- There is such a thing as attempting to *save life unlawfully.* That is when we commit some other sin in the process of sparing life. For example, if the choice is between denying Christ and sparing our life, it would be unlawful to deny Christ even if we were put to death for it. Nor is it ever lawful to tell a lie, even with a view to sparing life.
- There is also such a thing as *taking life lawfully.* That is when the authorities use capital punishment for a capital offence, or when there is loss of life on the aggressor's side in a just war, or when someone is killed in self-defence.

According to **Question 69**, the sixth commandment forbids anything which *"tendeth"* towards anyone losing their life unjustly. This prohibition covers a wide range of things, including:

- Sinful anger, hatred, desire for revenge,
- Hitting or wounding people,
- Immoderate sorrow, and excessive anxiety about our circumstances,
- Indifference to people's destitution and distress,
- Harming someone's trade or property when that is their means of maintaining life and health.

🔍 **Something to think about...**

- Why is murder so serious?
- When someone has a condition such as Parkinson's or Down's syndrome which means they will only ever have poor quality of life, people sometimes argue that it would be more merciful and dignified to allow them assistance to die. How is this view contradicted by the sixth commandment? Many babies who have Downs Syndrome are aborted in the womb because the parents do not want a child with this condition.
- In what way does it break the sixth commandment if you remain indifferent when you see someone in distress?

Personal reflection
How much effort do you put into preserving the life of your soul in comparison to preserving the life of your body?

How do we preserve purity?

When Joseph was sold by his brothers into slavery in Egypt, a man called Potiphar bought him. Some time later, Potiphar's wife tried to persuade Joseph to commit adultery with her (Genesis 39). We can think about what happened in Genesis 39 as a case study to help us understand the teaching of the seventh commandment.

70. Which is the seventh commandment?

A. The seventh commandment is, Thou shalt not commit adultery.

71. What is required in the seventh commandment?

A. The seventh commandment requireth the preservation of our own and our neighbour's chastity, in heart, speech and behaviour.

72. What is forbidden in the seventh commandment?

A. The seventh commandment forbiddeth all unchaste thoughts, words and actions.

Potiphar's wife breaking the seventh commandment

"Most forms of dancing encourage intimate physical contact or draw attention to our bodies, which also breaks the seventh commandment."

(a) Impure looks

When Potiphar's wife noticed that Joseph was well-built and handsome, she allowed this fact to prompt impure desires in her heart. It breaks the seventh commandment if we so much as look at someone with lustful intent (Matthew 5:28). Whether we see someone in real life, or recorded images in films, or videos, on social media, in magazines, or in adverts, we must preserve our chastity by refusing to look lustfully. *"I made a covenant with mine eyes; why then should I think upon a maid?"* (Job 31:1).

(b) Impure words

From thinking wrong things Potiphar's wife progressed to saying wrong things. She wanted what was wrong and she encouraged Joseph to also want what was wrong. She wanted Joseph to ignore the fact that she was married to Potiphar. Solomon gives an extended example in Proverbs 7 of the enticing suggestions which people make in order to flatter others into sinning with them against the seventh commandment. But in Ephesians 4:29 the Apostle Paul writes, *"Let no corrupt communication proceed out of your mouth."*

Other common forms of unchaste words which are forbidden by this commandment include obscene jokes, innuendo, and genres such as romance fiction. It is wrong to be entertained by such things whether or not we use such language ourselves (Romans 1:32; Ephesians 5:4; 1 Peter 4:3).

(c) Impure **actions**

Potiphar's wife did not stop at impure words but she actually took hold of Joseph in order to get him to sin with her. Men who touch women inappropriately are guilty of breaking the seventh commandment. Most forms of dancing encourage intimate physical contact or draw attention to our bodies, which also breaks the seventh commandment. Most people would acknowledge that someone forcing their unwanted attentions on somebody else is wrong, but the seventh commandment also forbids consensual impurity, whether between singles or married people, or men, or women.

Joseph keeping the seventh commandment

(a) Joseph **refused**

Joseph simply refused to join Potiphar's wife in committing adultery.

- If we are being tempted to break the seventh commandment, we should also simply refuse. We can simply refuse to watch notorious films and programmes; simply refuse to read notorious books; simply refuse to read lads' mags; simply refuse to look at porn.
- If we are being pressurised into behaviour which will compromise our chastity, we can simply refuse. If an attractive older man at work wants to take you for a coffee but you know he's married, simply refuse. If someone invites you to share compromising images of yourself

on social media, simply refuse. If your boyfriend or girlfriend doesn't understand the importance of waiting for marriage, simply refuse.

- Joseph simply refused, and he repeatedly refused. As the story unfolds, he ends up being falsely accused and unjustly punished as a consequence of acting with integrity. Whatever might be the social pressures, and whatever mockery and bullying might follow, faithfulness to the Lord, who is our God, and our Redeemer, should help us to constantly refuse to break the seventh commandment.

"The solution is never to commit adultery."

(b) Joseph **reasoned**

- *Joseph pointed out to Potiphar's wife that it would be completely inappropriate for him to sin in this way given his position.* He was in a position of great responsibility and trust, and committing adultery was totally incompatible with this.

Breaking the seventh commandment is always completely inappropriate, and especially, for someone in our position. As *human beings made in the image of God,* we should treat ourselves and others with more respect than to cheapen our bodies and souls by breaking the seventh commandment. But *the Lord is also our God and Redeemer.* If we have been brought up in a godly home, and if we are familiar with the Bible, then breaking the seventh commandment is even more sinful. If we have been baptised, then we are publicly identified as belonging to Christ, body and soul, and committing adultery is totally incompatible with this. If we have formally professed that Christ is our Saviour, then we are also claiming that our bodies are temples of the Holy Spirit. *"Know ye not that your bodies are members of Christ? ... the temple of the Holy Ghost?"* (1 Corinthians 6:15-20) Impurity should be completely out of the question for us.

- *Joseph pointed out to Potiphar's wife that she was married.*

  God ordained marriage to be between one man and one woman, to the exclusion of all others, for life. Sometimes people find themselves in unhappy or even abusive marriages, but the solution is never to commit adultery. It is exceptionally sinful for married people to break the seventh commandment because doing so violates what should be an exceptionally close and secure relationship, harming both themselves and the person they are married to. Married people should work together on their love and loyalty for each other, so that they continue to find all their delight in each other. Single people should also put a high value on other people's marriages.

  Single people should put a high value on their own chastity, and avoid resenting their singleness. Singleness is not second best, but an honourable calling in its own right. We're not incomplete or lacking in a worthwhile identity all the while we remain single.

- *Joseph pointed out to Potiphar's wife that what she was suggesting was a great wickedness, and a sin against God.* Resisting temptations to break the seventh commandment, on the other hand, is right in God's sight and we can ask Him for His help to do this in a way that is pleasing to Him. The more we focus on the holiness of God and the beauty of honouring Him, the less opportunity we will have to be distracted by the many temptations

which surround us to break the seventh commandment.

(c) Joseph **ran**

- Potiphar's wife spoke to Joseph day after day. But day after day, Joseph wouldn't listen to her, wouldn't consent to commit adultery with her, and wouldn't even be in her company. He took as many precautions as he could to safeguard himself from committing adultery and to reduce her opportunity to sin.

- Eventually, when there was nothing else to be done, Joseph ran away. That was the best and wisest thing he could do in the circumstances. Sometimes it's impossible to escape from someone who is determined to break the seventh commandment. Tamar would have run away from Amnon if it had been possible (2 Samuel 13). In a case like that, the sin of breaking the seventh commandment is completely on the side of the abuser, not on the victim. But where we can remove ourselves altogether from an environment where there is an imminent risk of the seventh commandment being broken, we should do so.

Purity in **an impure world**

Joseph lived in a very sinful time in the history of the world and so do we. Disregard for the seventh commandment is perhaps the defining sin of our generation. People no longer have the awareness that living together without being married breaks the seventh commandment. In spite of the very serious promises people make to stay together as husband and wife when they get married, many men leave their wives and many women leave their husbands because they meet someone else or simply feel it's time to move on. There is also widespread acceptance that marriage can be between two men or two women just as validly as between one man and one woman. Meanwhile all sorts of appalling abuse of children and vulnerable young people is coming to light. People are being pressurised into sexual activity at increasingly younger ages. Women are objectified and demeaned and need to be constantly on their guard against harassment even in public places.

> "Truly loving someone means that you respect their body as well as their soul."

Much of this can be attributed to blurring the distinction between love and lust. Potiphar's wife didn't love Joseph, and Amnon didn't love Tamar. Instead they were motivated by lust. Truly loving someone means that you respect their body as well as their soul. When people are married, their bodies belong to each other, so they should keep their bodies for each other. Single people have no right to think or act as though they have any claim on anyone else's body. They preserve their own and other people's chastity by supporting their married friends and respecting their unmarried friends.

Q Something to think about...

- When people reach their late teens and early twenties, it can sometimes feel that while the world pressurises you to be in a relationship, the church pressurises you to be married. How does the seventh commandment help you to be satisfied with singleness for as long as you remain unmarried?
- We typically feel disgusted and disappointed when someone we know cheats on their marriage partner. Our Lord and Redeemer regards unfaithfulness to Him as similar to unfaithfulness in marriage (e.g., Jeremiah 3). Whether you are married or unmarried, what can you do to guard your heart to be totally committed to the Lord?
- A lack of purity is destroying families in western societies. Children are born out of wedlock and grow up in broken families where their parents go from one partner to the next. How is purity essential to a society that is well-ordered?

How do we prosper in the right way?

So far we have seen that love to our neighbour expresses itself in respect for their status, respect for their life, and respect for their chastity. Now in the eighth commandment we turn to look at respect for our neighbour's possessions.

93. Which is the eighth commandment?

A. The eighth commandment is, Thou shalt not steal.

94. What is required in the eighth commandment?

A. The eighth commandment requireth the lawful procuring and furthering the wealth and outward estate of ourselves and others.

95. What is forbidden in the eighth commandment?

A. The eighth commandment forbiddeth whatsoever doth or may unjustly hinder our own or our neighbour's wealth or outward estate.

It is wrong to steal

The eighth commandment means that we are to get or *procure* our money and our possessions only by honest means. Unless somebody gives us something as a gift, with no strings attached, this commandment means that in order to have money and possessions we are to work. *"Let him that stole steal no more: but rather let him labour, working with his hands"* (Ephesians 4:28).

People who are unable to work because of disability, or caring for family members, need to be provided for through charity. This could be administered by the state (using taxes raised from those who work) or a voluntary organisation (using charitable donations from the general public) or by the church (using donations from church members), or it could come from personal goodwill on an individual basis. It is part of keeping the eighth commandment that when we can, we should freely give away our money and possessions to help people who are in need, especially if they are fellow believers (Galatians 6:10), but also including foreigners and temporary residents (Leviticus 25:35).

Keeping the eighth commandment also means that we are to take good care of the

"Keeping the eighth commandment also means that we are to take good care of the things we have and not to be careless or extravagant with our money or possessions."

things we have, and not to be careless or extravagant with our money or possessions. For example, we are not to gamble or take part in raffles. If a gambler wins, they are a thief because they have gained wealth without giving an equivalent value in return. If they lose, they have wasted their resources which the Lord provided to be used productively.

Ways we **steal**

There are many ways in which we can be guilty of breaking the eighth commandment.

(a) Theft **from God**
We steal from God when we use the skills and energy He gives us to live in rebellion against Him, instead of devoting ourselves and all that we have to His service. We steal from God when we hold back from giving Him our tithes and offerings (Malachi 3:8). We also steal from God when we hold back from giving Him the time He requires, specifically the one whole day in seven which He has set apart for Himself.

(b) Theft **in the workplace**
Obviously if we help ourselves to money from the till, or if we take things home which belong to our boss and use them without permission, we are guilty of breaking the eighth commandment by stealing from our employer. But also wasting time at work means we are guilty of theft because we are being paid to work.

It is also a sin against the eighth commandment when employers do not pay their employees a fair wage, or if they do not pay employees their wages in full, at the set time.

(c) Theft **from the poor**
This commandment also gives us a responsibility to care for the poor. We should do all we can to help and relieve those who are less well off than ourselves. If we do not care for them when we get the opportunity, we are guilty of breaking the eighth commandment.

(d) Theft **from the government**
Those who work are required to pay money to the government in taxes, which helps to run the country. Jesus said that we are to give to Caesar (a stand-in term for the government) what is due to Caesar (Matthew 22:21). If we cheat and try to avoid paying our taxes we are stealing what is not ours and are guilty before God.

> "Those who work are required to pay money to the government in taxes, which helps to run the country."

(e) Theft **from those around us**
If we buy something, we must pay a reasonable price for it. We are not to take advantage of the seller if we notice that they do not know the true value of the item for sale, or are so desperate to sell that they will accept any price no matter how little we offer. Nor should we buy things on credit, especially extravagant things which we could really do without, if we know all along that we are unlikely to be able to pay up eventually.

If we are doing the selling we are not to pretend that what we are selling is better than it really is. Nor should we sell things that induce people to spend money on what is in itself wrong (such as selling things that help people get away with breaking the law or selling lucky charms).

Apart from buying and selling, we are not to keep what does not belong to us. If we borrow we must always return. If we find something which someone has lost and keep it instead of returning it to the person who owns it, we are breaking the eighth commandment.

> "If we were more conscious of the kindness of the Lord in giving us what we've got, we would find it much easier to keep the eighth commandment than to break it."

Reasons not to steal

It's easy to break the eighth commandment for various reasons. Earning an honest wage is hard work, when we would rather relax. Generosity is hard, when we have to go without to make sure that others have the basics. Contentment is hard, when we see so many things we would like to have, that we don't have.

But there are plenty of weighty considerations to motivate us to keep the eighth commandment. We own nothing that hasn't come to us in the Lord's good providence. The Lord gave us all the skills we have; the Lord makes job opportunities available; the Lord preserves us from illness and accidents which would prevent us from earning a living; the Lord provides sources of financial support to help us through difficult times when we can't work, and so on. If we were more conscious of the kindness of the Lord in giving us what we've got, we would find it much easier to keep the eighth commandment than to break it.

🔍 Something to think about...

- What are the honest ways for people to obtain wealth and possessions? Think of your own skills, interests and experiences and the opportunities available to you in providence. How do these things combine to help you keep the eighth commandment?
- What can we learn from the eighth commandment about the ways we should and shouldn't use our money?
- What did Zacchaeus do when he repented of taking more than he should have? (See Luke 19.) In what ways is this a good example for us to follow?

How we preserve the truth

The ninth commandment tells us that loving our neighbour includes showing respect to their reputation, or more generally, promoting the truth.

76 Which is the ninth commandment?

A. The ninth commandment is, Thou shalt not bear false witness against thy neighbour.

77 What is required in the ninth commandment?

A. The ninth commandment requireth the maintaining and promoting of truth between man and man, and of our own and our neighbour's good name, especially in witness-bearing.

78 What is forbidden in the ninth commandment?

A. The ninth commandment forbiddeth whatsoever is prejudicial to truth, or injurious to our own or our neighbour's good name.

The father of liars

"Jesus said that Satan is a liar and the father of lies."

We read in Genesis about the first liar in the world. Satan appeared in the Garden of Eden and spoke to Eve and lied to her. Jesus said that Satan is a liar and the father of lies (John 8:44). What sort of lies does Satan tell?

- Sometimes the lie flatly contradicts the truth. *"Ye shall not surely die."* (Genesis 3:4)
- Sometimes the lie makes the truth seem doubtful. *"Does Job fear God for nought?"* (Job 1:9)
- Sometimes the lie includes a partial truth but conceals the whole truth to give a misleading impression. *"Why hath Satan filled thine heart to lie to the Holy Ghost, and to keep back part of the price?"* (Acts 5:3)

Until he sinned and became like the devil, Adam was only interested in the truth. When Adam fell, he, and everyone who came after him, began to listen to lies more than to the truth. People lie because they are sinners and because they are like Satan, the father of lies. How does our likeness to Satan show through?

"How easy it is to tell a lie to get us out of some difficulty!"

The frequency of lies

Our fundamental aversion to accepting the truth as God tells it, in turn gives rise to frequent disregard for the truth in our interactions with other people.

There are many different ways to break the ninth commandment. We break the ninth commandment when we tell deliberate lies. How easy it is to tell a lie to get us out of some difficulty! But we are to love the truth. A heart that loves the truth will bring forth the truth, whether it makes life easy for us or difficult. We must *maintain and promote the truth between each other.*

Another way of breaking the ninth commandment is by telling *'white lies.'* These are lies that we think don't really matter very much, or lies which we excuse because we tell them to avoid hurting someone's feelings. But something is either true or false, and if it is false it is a sin to say it. We are not to commit the evil of lying even with the intention that good may come of it.

Another way in which this commandment is frequently broken is when we make others believe something that is not true about someone. If we repeat little stories that are just not true we tell lies. Even if we repeat stories that might or might not be true, someone innocent could get a bad name. The best rule is never to start such stories, and never to spread them, because the ninth commandment requires us to maintain and promote *"our neighbour's good name".*

We also break this commandment if we deliberately put a misleading slant on things, either by boasting to make ourselves seem more important or clever, or by flattering other people.

On the other hand, we can also break this commandment by *saying what is strictly true but with malicious intent,* such as with the aim of provoking someone to be angry against someone else. Our aim should always be only to speak the truth in love.

We are not obliged under the ninth commandment *to tell everyone everything at all times.* For example, if a fraudster wants to know our bank account details, we are free to withhold that information from them. Or if we know personal details about someone's health condition, which they would prefer to keep private, we ought not say what we know to be true even if somebody asks us directly.

Nevertheless, there are other circumstances *when silence can be as bad as speaking.* We must not conceal the truth with the intent to deceive, and neither should we keep quiet for selfish reasons when questions of justice are at stake. For example, if someone is accused of doing something wrong and we know they did not do it, we should speak up and tell the truth, so that the innocent are not punished unjustly and so that the guilty do not go free.

"We are not obliged under the ninth commandment to tell everyone everything at all times."

The future of liars

Perhaps for a time we can get away with telling lies without the truth becoming known. But God often has ways of bringing the truth out. When Joseph's brothers sold him into slavery and pretended to Jacob their father that he had been killed by a wild animal, their lie was undetected for a long time. But God eventually brought things around in such a way that Jacob and everyone else knew that they had lied.

Not every lie is exposed in this world but on the day of judgment every single lie will be judged. There is a very solemn verse in Revelation which says that *"all liars shall have their part in the lake which burneth with fire and brimstone" (Revelation 21:8).* If we are to escape this punishment, we have to believe the truth of God's Word and accept salvation in Jesus Christ, who is the way, the truth, and the life.

🔍 Something to think about...

- Does it only break the ninth commandment if you flatly contradict the truth?
- Why is it so important for preachers to tell the truth when they are preaching?

Personal reflection
How fully do you accept the truth of God's verdict on your sinfulness? How wholeheartedly do you accept the truth of God's recommendation of Christ as the Saviour for sinners like you?

How can we be content?

The tenth commandment focuses on our respect for our neighbour's situation. Instead of coveting their position or their belongings, we should be pleased when they do well, and content with what we ourselves have.

79 Which is the tenth commandment?

A. The tenth commandment is, Thou shalt not covet thy neighbour's house, thou shalt not covet thy neighbour's wife, nor his man-servant, nor his maidservant, nor his ox, nor his ass, nor any thing that is thy neighbour's.

80 What is required in the tenth commandment?

A. The tenth commandment requireth full contentment with our own condition, with a right and charitable frame of spirit toward our neighbour and all that is his.

81 What is forbidden in the tenth commandment?

A . The tenth commandment forbiddeth all discontentment with our own estate, envying or grieving at the good of our neighbour, and all inordinate motions and affections to any thing that is his.

What does covetousness look like?

Covetousness is the opposite of contentment. A contented person is happy with what they've got, whatever they may lack; and when they look at other people they're pleased when others prosper and sympathetic when they suffer.

"The covetous person is discontented with their life and they always want more than they have."

The covetous person is discontented with their life and they always want more than they have. The covetous person is also jealous of what others have and always wants these things for himself. Instead of being happy when others are better off, the covetous person feels envious and annoyed.

In 1 Kings 21 we read about the covetousness of Ahab. Ahab was the king, and near his palace was a vineyard belonging to a man called Naboth. Ahab decided that he would like Naboth's vineyard, so he offered to buy it from him. When Naboth turned down the offer, Ahab went home in such a sullen temper that he refused to eat. What did Ahab's covetousness look like?

- **Ahab didn't need Naboth's vineyard.** He was the king, and had all sorts of lands at his disposal. He only wanted Naboth's because of its convenient location and so that he could grow some vegetables on the side.
- **Ahab didn't care about Naboth's welfare.** This land was precious to Naboth because it was part of his family's inheritance in the promised land of Israel. So no amount of cash would have compensated Naboth for the loss of it. This land would also have been necessary to Naboth, as he presumably made his living from working it as a vineyard.
- **Ahab was intensely and disproportionately annoyed that he couldn't have what he wanted.** He could have decided, on reflection, that he already had plenty. Instead, he gave wicked Jezebel a free pass to engineer that Naboth would be falsely accused and unjustly executed. He then helped himself to the vineyard once Naboth was dead.

In Romans 7:7, Paul confesses that he was previously a covetous person. But Paul's covetousness looked very different from Ahab's.

- **Paul was completely respectable.** Unlike Ahab, Paul was no irreligious monarch subject to his own whims, but an exceptionally upright Jew with an impeccable pedigree among the people of God.
- **Paul kept all the law outwardly.** He lived according to the strictest variety of Judaism available. Out of zeal for God he persecuted those who he regarded as defiling true religion, and as far as anyone could tell, he was completely blameless in keeping the law. He certainly never perverted the course of justice, or arranged for someone to be murdered or callously took possession of a poor man's inheritance.
- **Paul didn't realise that God looked at the heart.** Until God started to work in his heart, he didn't even realise that he was guilty of covetousness.

Whether the discontent and envy of our hearts work themselves out in practical ways for anyone to see, or whether we manage to carefully suppress our impulses to act on them, our heart sins are still sinful. If we grudge against people who are cleverer than us, or better at sport, or more popular, we are breaking the tenth commandment. If we resent it when we see someone with a bigger house, a nicer car, a better model of phone, a higher paid job, or more exotic holidays, we are breaking the tenth commandment.

Why is covetousness **wrong?**

(a) Covetousness implies that God is not good.
God is good when He gives us what we have, and God is good when he withholds from us the things we don't have. The covetous person, by grieving over their situation and harbouring bitterness over what they don't have, behaves as if God has not been good to them, or not as good as He could have been. They think that if God was really good He would have made them more richer or more gifted than they are and given them better circumstances.

(b) Covetousness implies that God is not wise.
God knew what He was doing when He made us as we are and when He gave us what we have. If we are covetous we think we are wiser than God, because if we had our way we would do things differently and better.

How can covetousness **be cured?**

One cure for covetousness is not to have all our hopes and desires on the things of this world. *"A man's life consisteth not in the abundance of the things which he possesseth"* (Luke 12:15). If we set our heart on things that really matter — the possession of spiritual blessings and an expectation of spending eternity with God in heaven — then we will see our worldly possessions and circumstances in the right perspective. Then when we see adverts for a glamorous lifestyle, we don't need to take them too seriously, and when our friends have an easy and successful life, we will be free to celebrate this with them. We should also pray that the Lord would make us happy and content with what we have; and if by hard work and wise use of our abilities He grants us more and better than we already have, we can accept it thankfully as a blessing from the Lord, without wasting our energy on constantly craving after it.

To keep covetousness in check, we should also remember not only that God has been good to us but that, as sinners, we deserve nothing. It is right and lawful to be ambitious and want to use the gifts God has given to the best of our abilities and for His glory. We should seek to improve our condition in life. But we need to do this in a way that is not covetous and discontented. If we were more humble we would be less covetous. When the Lord Jesus was on the earth, He said, *"Foxes have holes, and birds of the air have nests; but the Son of Man hath not where to lay his head"* (Luke 9:58). If the Lord of glory was content in such deprived circumstances, how dare we complain? When we have problems and things are not going so well for us, rather than grumbling and complaining and wishing that things were different, we should see our circumstances as God's perfect will for us.

We should repent of our covetousness and find forgiveness for it. We have to find the complete satisfaction of our hearts in Christ Jesus and in the blood of Christ cleansing us from this sin. If we are born again, the Lord will become the best and most precious thing we possess. If we have eternal life through Jesus Christ, we have something which cannot be improved on. Whatever else we may lack, if we can say that the Lord is our shepherd then we *"shall not want"* (Psalm 23).

> "To keep covetousness in check, we should also remember not only that God has been good to us but that, as sinners, we deserve nothing."

🔍 Something to think about...

- How is it possible to be content in your limited and ordinary circumstances when you see other people with their huge houses, expensive possessions, and highly paid jobs?
- How is it possible to want a promotion at work without breaking the tenth commandment?

Personal reflection

Different things appeal to different people. Some people covet money, some people covet status, others covet academic success, others covet popularity, and so on. What sort of things do you find the most attractive, which you are therefore particularly in danger of coveting?

Can we keep God's commandments?

In Questions 39 to 81 we have been looking at what God requires us to do. The broadest answer is that we have to do God's will (Questions 39 and 40). We have now narrowed this down into specific requirements by looking at the Ten Commandments (Questions 41 to 81). But there is a problem. Is anyone actually able to keep these commandments?

> **82** Is any man able perfectly to keep the commandments of God?
>
> A. No mere man since the fall is able, in this life, perfectly to keep the commandments of God, but doth daily break them in thought, word and deed.

"God gave us His law to love it and keep it. It is the rule by which we are to live our lives in this world."

Beautiful commandments

Looking at the Ten Commandments has shown us that God's moral law ranges wide and deep. The law is a very beautiful standard. It reflects the beauty of God's own holiness. It is *"holy, and just, and good"* (Romans 7:12).

God gave us His law to love it and keep it. It is the rule by which we are to live our lives in this world. The moral law, as well as being beautiful, is binding. It is perpetually binding. There is never a time when we are not obliged to obey it. It is also universally binding. Everybody is under obligation to obey it. The fact that we are sinners does not remove our obligation to keep God's commandments perfectly. Nor does the fact that God loves and saves His people remove their obligation to keep His commandments perfectly.

Broken commandments

But nobody is able to keep God's commandments perfectly. We are all mere humans, and fallen humans, and *"no mere man since the fall"* is able to keep God's law. We are *not able,* not just because we are too weak, but because we are too sinful. Our inability is sinful inability. It is our own sin that makes us unable to keep the commandments. Certainly, before the fall, Adam was capable of keeping God's law, but after the fall that all changed. Certainly too, the Lord Jesus Christ kept God's commandments perfectly. But He was not a mere man, although He was a real man. And certainly, in the life to come, when Christ takes His people to glory, they will be able to keep God's commandments perfectly. But not *"in this life."*

Instead, we break God's commandments *"daily,"* or continually. We break them *"in thought, word and deed."* Being unable to keep the commandments does not mean that we do nothing. It means that we actively *"break them,"* either by neglecting what is our duty, or by doing what is forbidden.

Q **Something to think about...**

*   What are the daily implications of Adam's fall for your life?
*   How is it fair for God to be angry with us for failing to keep the law if we are unable to?
*   Since we cannot obey perfectly, does this mean we don't need to try to obey?

Are some sins worse than others?

We are all continually breaking God's law. It is wicked to break God's law in any way. But is everything we do equally wicked? This is the topic of Question 83.

> **83** Are all transgressions of the law equally heinous?
>
> A. Some sins in themselves, and by reason of several aggravations, are more heinous in the sight of God than others.

Some sins are worse than other sins

If something is *"heinous"* it is wicked and hateful to God. God sees every instance of breaking His law as something heinous. But in God's eyes, are all transgressions of His law equally heinous? Question 83 says no. There are degrees, or levels, of wickedness. Some

"It is worse to sin against God than against other people."

sins are more heinous than others *"in themselves,"* that is, in their own nature or just because of what they are. For example, it is worse to sin against God than against other people. It is worse to worship an idol or use the name of God in vain, than it is to steal or tell a lie. Of the sins that we commit against other people, some are worse than others. For example, it is worse to murder someone than it is to steal from someone.

Some sinning is worse than other sinning

God judges some acts of sin as worse than others depending on the details of how they were committed. Sins can be characterised by *"several aggravations,"* or various different things that make them more serious.

(a) Sins are aggravated by **the person who commits them**
Your sin is worse the older and more experienced you are, the better your reputation is, and the more likely it is that other people will follow your example.

(b) Sins are aggravated by **those whom the sin is committed against**
Your sin is worse if it is committed directly against any person of the Godhead. It is worse the more senior the person is to you, the closer you are to them, and the more vulnerable they are. It is worse to sin against people's souls than their bodies, and worse to sin against many people than a few.

(c) Sins are aggravated by **the ingredients of the sin committed**

Your sin is worse if it is explicitly forbidden in the law, or breaks more than one commandment at a time, or if it erupts from your thoughts into words and actions. It is worse if you do it when you know better, or against your own conscience, or when you have been warned against it. It is worse if you do it deliberately, boldly, maliciously, or frequently.

(d) Sins are aggravated by **the circumstances they are committed**

Your sin is worse if it is committed on the Lord's day, or during or around a time of worship. It is worse if it is done in public, or in the presence of those who are likely to be grieved or harmed by it.

Q Something to think about...

- Looking at the four categories of *'aggravation,'* can you identify what makes one sin worse than another in the following examples?

  - Aaron's sin compared to the sin of the Israelites in general when they made the golden calf (Exodus 32).
  - Peter's sin compared to the sin of the other Jews and Barnabas when they withdrew from the Gentile believers (Galatians 2:11-14).
  - The sin of someone who steals from a friend who has always been kind to them, compared to someone who steals from a stranger.
  - The sin of someone who drives recklessly on a busy motorway, causing a multiple vehicle pile-up where many people are badly injured, compared to someone who collides with another car at low speed in a supermarket car park.
  - The sin of someone who has been brought up to know the Bible in a God-fearing family, compared to their friend who doesn't have a Christian upbringing, when they don't attend church and lead a worldly lifestyle.

What does sin deserve?

We all sin all the time (Question 82) and some of our sins are worse than others (Question 83). We turn now to look at what our sins deserve.

> **84** What doth every sin deserve?
>
> A. Every sin deserveth God's wrath and curse, both in this life, and that which is to come.

"Every sin is heinous. Even the smallest sin is contrary to God."

Every sin is heinous

Every sin is heinous. Even the smallest sin is contrary to God. It is against *God's sovereignty,* asserting our own will and authority over God's will and authority. It is against *God's goodness,* fighting His kindness with our badness and ingratitude. It is against *God's holiness,* contradicting His purity with our corruption and pollution. It is against *God's righteous law,* violating His perfect standard with our non-compliance and transgression. All this is true for the tiniest and most insignificant sin you can imagine. Some sins are more heinous than others, but even the least heinous sin is absolutely evil.

God is right to be angry

Every sin, even the least, deserves God's anger, here called His **"wrath."** The only possible response God can give to any sin is anger. God's anger is not an emotion, like our anger, which comes and goes, and flares up sometimes for no real reason. God's anger is His consistent and permanent aversion to evil (much like His love is His consistent and permanent pleasure in what is holy). Wherever there is evil, God is necessarily angry. Our sins deserve that God is angry with us, both in this life, and in the life to come.

God is right to punish sin

Every sin, even the least, deserves to be punished. The **"curse"** of God is the expression of His anger in a punishment, in particular the penalty of the broken covenant. If God's wrath is His attitude towards sinners, God's curse is His attitude put into action against them. As we saw in Question 19, the penalty of the broken law includes **"all miseries in this life,... death itself, and ... the pains of hell for ever."**

Sometimes people wonder why sin deserves a punishment of such magnitude. Considering that sins are committed by puny, finite humans, and a sin can sometimes be over and done with in just a moment of time, why does sin deserve *all* miseries, *for ever*? But we have to measure the magnitude of sin by the God we sin against. Sin deserves infinite punishment because it is against God's infinite holiness. The wrath and curse of God now and for ever is not a disproportionate response to our sins. It is only what we deserve.

🔍 **Something to think about...**

• What is the smallest sin you can imagine? Why is it still not actually that small?

Personal reflection
Death is called the wages of sin (Romans 6:23). It is both the inevitable consequence of sin, and exactly what we have earned. Does this strike you as a fair wage for your sin?

How can we escape God's wrath?

We have to understand our problem. God's wrath and curse is simply what we deserve for our sin. We sin all the time, and we are too sinful to stop sinning. All we can do is treasure up more and more wrath. Is there any way to escape the dreadful punishment that is inexorably coming our way?

> **85** What doth God require of us, that we may escape his wrath and curse due to us for sin?
>
> A. To escape the wrath and curse of God due to us for sin, God requireth of us faith in Jesus Christ, repentance unto life, with the diligent use of all the outward means whereby Christ communicateth to us the benefits of redemption.

> "Punishment is coming our way deservedly, but a way of escape is opened up graciously."

What we **don't deserve**

Punishment is coming our way *deservedly,* but a way of escape is opened up *graciously.* We do not deserve to escape. Escape is not **"due to us,"** unlike God's wrath and curse. The fact that a way of escape exists at all is entirely because of God's grace (or, as Question 20 called it, **"His mere good pleasure"**). Everything about the way of escape is God's own provision. As we have already seen in Questions 20 to 38, it is God who planned salvation, God who purchased salvation, and God who applies salvation. Pursued by God's righteous indignation, and with nothing at all to offer in our own defence, when we get a glimpse of a way of escape, we can only explain it by God's grace.

What we **must do**

God, who provides salvation, requires something from us. Question 85 tells us that God requires three things - *faith, repentance, and use of the means of grace.* We will look at each of these in turn in the remaining questions of the Catechism. For now, there are three things we have to understand about these requirements.

(a) God requires that we must do these things

These are activities and behaviours that nobody else can do for us - not even Christ, not even the Spirit, and clearly not anyone else on our behalf. If I don't believe, don't repent, and don't use the means of grace, then I will not escape the wrath and curse of God due to me for sin. In fact, my unbelief, my impenitence, and my neglect of the means are themselves sins which deserve their own punishment.

(b) God requires these things as **the means, not the basis, of escape**

The basis of salvation is Christ's satisfaction. It is Christ who has earned our salvation by His obedience and death. Our faith and repentance can never earn us salvation. God requires them on our part only as instruments or channels of receiving the redemption He provides.

(c) God requires these things as **instruments, not works**

They are not things that He requires us to produce by ourselves, as if some part of our salvation depends on works that we have to do. People sometimes talk as if God lets us off without perfect obedience if only we believe. But this only substitutes one kind of work (obedience), with another kind of work (faith), and salvation is not of works. Faith, repentance and grace are gifts that God provides us as part of the gift of salvation. They are required as connecting links between us and the blessings of salvation, not as if God will only accept us on account of our personal performance of them.

Q **Something to think about...**

- Why does a way of escape exist when we deserve only the opposite?
- People sometimes reason like this, *'If God wants me to be saved, He will give me faith. I can't be responsible if God doesn't give me faith.'* What is wrong with this way of thinking?
- Our faith, repentance, and use of the means do not earn us salvation. Why are they still essential requirements of salvation?

What is faith?

We turn now to look in detail at what we must do if we are to be saved. The first thing to look at is faith in Jesus Christ.

This is not the first time the Catechism has mentioned faith. In Question 30 we saw that the Holy Spirit gives us faith as the means of uniting us to Christ. In Question 31 we saw that the Spirit enables us to believe, described as embracing Jesus Christ. In Question 33 we saw that faith is the instrument which receives Christ's righteousness for justification. Here in Question 86 the Catechism offers us a definition of faith from the perspective of what we are required to do to escape the wrath and curse of God due to us for sin.

86 What is faith in Jesus Christ?

A. Faith in Jesus Christ is a saving grace, whereby we receive and rest upon him alone for salvation, as he is offered to us in the gospel.

"We must come and put our trust in the person of Christ as a Saviour for ourselves."

Faith is **in Jesus Christ**

The faith which saves is a faith which focusses on Jesus Christ.

Christ **Himself**

The Bible tells us many facts about Christ, which we must believe. It tells us that God the Father sent His Son the Lord Jesus Christ to live and die as the substitute for sinners. It tells us that after He died this atoning death, He rose again, and that He is coming back on the last day. But it is not enough just to believe these things as facts. Although we can assent to facts, we must entrust ourselves to a person, the person of Christ. Nor is it enough to want the benefits of salvation, without caring about the Saviour Himself. We must come and put our trust in the person of Christ as a Saviour for ourselves.

Christ **alone**

We are to trust in Jesus Christ *"alone"* for salvation. We must not try to trust in Christ and something else. We are not saved by trusting partly to Christ and partly to our own works or efforts to please God. Salvation is *"not of works, lest any man should boast"* (Ephesians 2:9). The Bible speaks of our attempts at good works, which we hope will please God, not as something which will help to save us, but actually as things which God sees as *"filthy rags"* (Isaiah 64:6). When the prison keeper in Philippi asked the apostle Paul how he could be saved, Paul answered, *"Believe on the Lord Jesus Christ, and thou shalt be saved"* (Acts 16:31).

Christ **for salvation**

We are to believe in Jesus Christ *"for salvation."* We must not imagine that Christ will give us a passport to heaven, and otherwise leave us free to continue sinning. If Christ is our Saviour, He saves us from sin. He will not save us and leave us in our sins. He will not save us along with our favourite sins. He will not save us so that we can sin all the more. When we come to Christ, we have to desire the actual salvation which He provides, salvation from both the guilt of sin and the defilement of sin. The purpose of His saving work is, *"that he might redeem us from all iniquity, and purify unto himself a peculiar people, zealous of good works"* (Titus 2:14).

Faith is **receiving and resting**

What is meant by faith in Jesus Christ? The Catechism describes it as *"receiving and resting"* on Him.

> "Each believer gets a whole and complete Saviour."

- We must *receive* Him – as He is the gift of God. We can't earn this gift or pay it back. We have to accept with thankfulness the very Saviour whom God has provided.
- We must *rest* on Him – as He is completely trustworthy. We can lay the full weight of responsibility for our soul's everlasting salvation on Him with the greatest confidence and satisfaction.

The Catechism says further that we receive and rest on Jesus Christ *"as he is offered to us in the gospel."* How is Jesus Christ offered to us in the gospel?

- *As exactly what we need.* If we are thirsty, Christ is offered as wine and milk (Isaiah 55:1). If we are hungry, Christ is offered as the bread of life (John 6:35). If we are poor and blind and naked, Christ offers gold and eye salve and white raiment (Revelation 3:18).
- *Wholly.* Even when thousands of people put their faith in Christ simultaneously, Christ is not shared out a part to each. Each believer gets a whole and complete Saviour. He is prophet, priest, and king to each believer. *"Christ Jesus ... is made unto us wisdom, and righteousness, and sanctification, and redemption"* (1 Corinthians 1:30).
- *Particularly.* Jesus Christ is offered to each individual sinner who encounters the gospel, as God's freely provided and completely trustworthy Saviour, and exactly the Saviour we need. As surely as each of us is obliged to accept the requirements of the law as applying to us individually and personally, so each of us is obliged to accept the offer of Christ in the gospel as applying to us individually and personally.

Faith is **a saving grace**

A grace **that saves us**

Faith saves us as the instrument by which we make contact with Christ. Although faith has no merit of its own, and although Christ is the object of our faith, and although the Spirit must enable us to have faith, yet without faith, we cannot escape the wrath and curse of God due to us for sin. But if we have faith, whatever other problems we have, and whatever else we lack, we will be saved. *"As Moses lifted up the serpent in the wilderness, even so must the Son of man be lifted up: that whosoever believeth in him should not perish, but have eternal life"* (John 3:14-15).

A grace **we must exercise**

Faith is not something that anyone else can do on our behalf. Our parents cannot believe on our behalf. We will not be saved by the faith of our godly friends. If we are going to be saved, we ourselves must personally receive and rest on Christ. Refusing to receive and rest on Christ leaves us guilty of unbelief; and as long as we persist in the sin of unbelief, we cannot be saved.

> "It is a great kindness on the part of the Lord when He brings a sinner to trust in Christ for salvation."

A grace **we must be given**

It is the Holy Spirit who makes us able to believe the promise of God's Word and trust in Christ. We need this work of the Spirit because by nature we are sinfully unable to put our trust in Christ, as we have already seen in Questions 30 and 31. The Lord in His mercy makes us able to trust in Him. As the Bible says, faith is *"the gift of God"* (Ephesians 2:8). It is a great kindness on the part of the Lord when He brings a sinner to trust in Christ for salvation. It is a kindness that we just do not deserve.

🔍 **Something to think about...**

- *'It's not faith that saves, it's Christ that saves.'* How far do you agree with this?
- Faith is something that God has to give you, you can't produce it by yourself. How should this fact make you humble? How should this fact give you hope?
- Why is unbelief such a serious sin?

What is repentance?

If we are to be saved, then along with faith and the use of the outward means, we must repent. What does repentance involve?

> **87** What is repentance unto life?
>
> A. Repentance unto life is a saving grace, whereby a sinner, out of a true sense of his sin, and apprehension of the mercy of God in Christ, doth, with grief and hatred of his sin, turn from it unto God, with full purpose of, and endeavour after, new obedience.

A new understanding of sin

It is part of our sinfulness to lack a true understanding of what sin is and what it means to be a sinner. We do not repent until we have *"a true sense of ... sin."* The true understanding of sin has two aspects. We realise for the first time the *danger* of our sin – it leaves us wide open to being lost for ever. But that is not the only problem with our sin. We also realise the *filthiness* of our sin, how disgusting it is, and how offensive it is to God. *"Against thee, thee only, have I sinned, and done this evil in thy sight"* (Psalm 51:4).

A new appreciation of Christ

Alongside a true sense of sin, we need a new *"apprehension of the mercy of God in Christ."* Here, 'apprehension' means a grasp or an appreciation. If we only understand that God is angry with sinners, we will be too fearful and resentful to turn towards Him in repentance. We must also grasp and understand that God has mercy on sinners for Christ's sake. We need a new appreciation of Christ as the Saviour of

> "Let the wicked forsake his way, and the unrighteous man his thoughts." (Isaiah 55:7)

sinners before we will repent. We need to grasp that Christ came *"to save sinners"* (1 Timothy 1:15), and that while we were still sinners, *"Christ died for us"* (Romans 5:8). The mercy of God and the love of Christ highlight the outrageous ingratitude of our sinfulness. But it is because of Christ that God's mercy flows out to people whose sins are as dangerous and disgusting as can be. Grasping and appreciating this, we have confidence to turn towards God in repentance.

A new direction

In repentance a sinner *turns from his sin.* When Isaiah calls us to repentance he says, *"Let the wicked forsake his way, and the unrighteous man his thoughts"* (Isaiah 55:7).

This turning is characterised by *grief for our sin.* When someone repents, their sins make them sorry, not only because of the consequences of their sin but also because of the sin itself. Naturally when people are afraid of punishment for doing something wrong, this makes them worried and sad. But people are not always particularly sorry about what they have done — they are just sorry that they have been caught and have consequences to face. If we are turning from our sin in repentance it will be marked by mourning because of our sin itself, because it of how it dishonours God.

This turning is also characterised by *hatred for our sin.* A little girl was told by her mother to pray that God would take away the sin in her heart. But she replied that she did not wish to pray for that as she liked her sin. *'It is rather nice,'* she said! That is just how we all feel by nature — we like our sin and we are content to remain sinners. We never really come to hate our sin until God shows us how ugly and offensive it is. **"Know therefore and see that it is an evil thing and bitter, that thou hast forsaken the LORD thy God"** (Jeremiah 2:19).

> "Repentance includes a full purpose to obey God, a whole-hearted resolve and determination."

In repentance a sinner *turns from his sin unto God.* It is not enough to turn from our sins. Isaiah's call to repentance did not stop at the requirement to forsake our sin. We are also urged, **"Let him return unto the LORD, and he will have mercy upon him; and to our God, for he will abundantly pardon"** (Isaiah 55:7). Turning towards God is what distinguishes true **"repentance unto life"** from the false repentance *'unto death.'* People can have a false repentance where they feel ashamed of their sins and resolve to do better. But because they never really take God into account, they really only turn from one kind of sinning to another kind of sinning. In true repentance, we turn from sin to God. In particular, we turn to God in Christ. God is the One who is offended by our sin. But God is only approachable by sinners as He makes Himself available in Christ.

A new way to live

Our turning to God in repentance is distinguished not only by grief and hatred for our sin, but also by **"full purpose of, and endeavour after, new obedience."** Someone who has found the mercy of God in Christ will be eternally thankful to God. This thankfulness will express itself in a desire to obey Him.

Repentance includes a **"full purpose"** to obey God, a whole-hearted resolve and determination. We will have every intention of obeying God in every way. And not only good intentions — we also **"endeavour after"** obedience. We effortfully, diligently, strive to obey Him. We not only aspire to be obedient but we try to achieve it.

This obedience is a new way of life. It is not just a one-off, but something we continue in throughout the whole of the rest of our lives. It is a constant serious effort to live a righteous life.

In what way is our obedience **"new"** once we repent?

- It flows from a new principle — the principle of faith and love
- It is influenced by new motives — the grace of God and the love of Christ
- It is performed in a new manner — in the strength of Christ, with pleasure, with

thankfulness, and with the whole heart
- It aims at a new goal — the glory of God

We see an example of this in the life of Zacchaeus. When Zacchaeus encountered the mercy of God in Christ, the genuineness of his repentance showed itself most obviously in the area of his biggest sin. Where he had wrongly extorted people's money or belongings, he restored it to them. Instead of keeping his riches for himself, he donated half his goods to the poor.

🔍 Something to think about...

- What are the two aspects of a *'true'* sense of sin?
- What is the difference between a *true* sense of sin and a *deep* sense of sin? Is a *deep* sense of sin necessary if we are to repent?
- If you get a sense of the mercy of God in Christ, how does this encourage you to forsake your sins? How does it encourage you to turn to God? How does it make you even more sorry for your sin?

Personal reflection
In Psalm 119 the psalmist says, **"I thought on my ways, and turned my feet unto thy testimonies"** (verse 59). Have you ever reflected on your own behaviour, habits, and preferences in a way that has made you leave your own path and instead take the path of God's Word? The psalmist adds, **"I made haste, and delayed not"** (verse 60). Has the need to leave your sin and find God in Christ become something urgent to you; something you can't delay?

What means do we need to use?

We saw from Question 85 that God requires three things from us if we are to be saved. Now that we have looked at faith (Question 86) and repentance (Question 87), we turn to the means of grace. Here in Question 88 we are given a list of three special means of grace - the Word, the sacraments, and prayer.

> **88** What are the outward means whereby Christ communicateth to us the benefits of redemption?
>
> A. The outward and ordinary means whereby Christ communicateth to us the benefits of redemption, are his ordinances, especially the word, sacraments and prayer; all which are made effectual to the elect for salvation.

We must know about the means

The *"benefits of redemption"* are what Christ has purchased for His people. As we saw in Questions 32 to 38, Christ provides every possible spiritual blessing in this life and in the life to come. These include justification, sanctification, adoption, and all the further blessings which accompany or flow from these, as well as perfection in holiness, resurrection to honour, and the full enjoying of God to all eternity. In summary, the blessings of redemption are union and communion with God in Christ through the Spirit.

But how does Christ bestow the blessings of salvation on sinners? He *"communicateth,"* or bestows, or gives the benefits of redemption through the *means of grace,* here referred to as His *"ordinances."*

> "... the blessings of redemption are union and communion with God in Christ through the Spirit."

Christ has many *"outward and ordinary"* ordinances. They include meditation on the Word, thanksgiving, church government, fasting, oaths and vows, among others. However, there are three ordinances He uses *"especially"* to give us the benefits of redemption. These are *"the word, sacraments, and prayer."* These three are what is normally meant when we speak of *the means of grace.*

- These are called the *"outward"* means because there is something visible, tangible, or physical about them. They are distinct from the *inward* means, whether referring to our inward activities (such as faith and repentance), or the inward activities of the Holy Spirit (such as regeneration and assurance).

- They are also called *"ordinary"* means, because they are what God uses in all normal cases. In extraordinary situations, He is not limited to using these means. If He is going to save someone who is unable to understand the Word or participate in the sacraments (for example, an infant or someone with learning disabilities) then He is free to use extraordinary means. For everyone else, however, the ordinary means are what He has provided for us to use with diligence, if we are to be saved.

If God has provided these ways, or means, for us to receive the blessings of salvation, certain things follow on from that.

We must not despise the means

Because of sin we are very liable to despise the means of grace - the very things which God has ordained to communicate **"to us the benefits of redemption."** By these ordinances He actually conveys these blessings to us and puts us in possession of them.

We must not despise the Word, for **"faith cometh by hearing, and hearing by the word of God"** (Romans 10:17). We must not despise the sacraments, which show us in a visible form what we hear about in the Word. We must not despise prayer, which gives us access to God for all the blessings derived from Word and sacraments.

Nevertheless, some people say, *"I do not need to go to church in order to be saved. I can get all the blessings I need by meditating at home on my own, or going for a walk in the hills."* They are really saying that they will decide what the best means of getting God's blessings are. By despising the means God provides in

> "We must not despise the sacraments, which show us in a visible form what we hear about in the Word."

favour of their own, they are claiming that they know better than God and dictating to God how they think He should bestow His gifts on them.

We are also guilty of despising the means if we think that we will never be converted by the ordinary preaching of the Word of God, and instead wait for an extraordinary experience like the Apostle Paul on the Damascus Road. If we keep looking for something new and different, or if we are never satisfied with the minister we have, though we know he preaches the truth, then we are in danger of despising God's means. The Catechism teaches us that God's blessing is not to be expected in the unusual but in the ordinary means of grace.

We must not neglect the means

Many who do not despise the means of grace are nevertheless guilty of neglecting them. Satan is always busy and very cunning. If you have been brought up in a Christian home, or in a good church, he may not try to turn you totally against the things of God. Instead, he will try to get you to put them to one side, and not think about them. He will discourage church attendance, Bible reading and prayer; or encourage you to use them in only a sloppy and half-hearted way.

But these are the means which God has especially ordained to be *"effectual ... for salvation."* Instead of neglecting them, we must use them with diligence. We must pay attention to the message of the Word when we read it or hear it preached. We must understand the significance of the sacraments, and participate in them conscientiously. We must pray thoughtfully and in sincerity. We cannot expect to be saved if we neglect these means.

We must not trust in the means

God's ordinances are only means. We must use them, but we must not trust in them to save us. They have to be *"made effectual"* to salvation. They are not automatically effective, they are made effective by the Spirit.

We must never think that we will be automatically saved because we read our Bibles or because we were baptised. God's ordinances are means, or channels, or methods of allowing grace to come from God and reach us. They are not an end in themselves.

As we use the means, we always have to aim for the spiritual blessings themselves (the actual *"benefits of redemption"*), and we always have to rely on the Spirit to grant us these blessings.

We have a practical illustration of this in Acts chapter 2. In verse 42 Luke records that *"they continued stedfastly in the apostles' doctrine and fellowship, and in breaking of bread, and in prayers."* These are the outward and ordinary means which we have been speaking of. Then several verses further down in the chapter we see the Lord using and blessing these very means for the conversion of souls: *"the Lord added to the church daily such as should be saved"* (verse 47).

"We must pray thoughtfully and in sincerity."

Q **Something to think about...**

- How highly do you value the benefits of redemption? Are you prepared to be diligent about obtaining these benefits by using the very means which Christ has appointed?
- Think of the many people who don't go to church. They don't know the Word, don't participate in the sacraments, and don't pray. Why is their situation desperate? What can we do to help them?

How does the Bible change us?

The ordinary means of receiving the blessings of salvation are the Word, sacraments, and prayer. We turn now to look at each of these in more detail, beginning with the Word. The Catechism devotes two questions to the Word as a means of grace. Question 89 asks how the Spirit uses the Word, and in Question 90 we will see how we should use the Word.

89 How is the Word made effectual to salvation?

A. The Spirit of God maketh the reading, but especially the preaching of the Word, an effectual means of convincing and converting sinners, and of building them up in holiness and comfort, through faith, unto salvation.

Reading and hearing the Word

"The word" is the Bible, the Scriptures of the Old and New Testaments (as we saw in Question 2). There are two ways of encountering the Word of God. One way is by *"reading"* it. If we are to benefit from the Word we must read it. The Bible is written for ordinary people, and is not reserved for specialist scholars or only the holiest of religious people. Everyone is permitted and expected to read God's Word, both on their own, and in their families.

> "The Bible is written for ordinary people, and is not reserved for specialist scholars or only the holiest of religious people."

It is *"the Spirit of God"* who makes the reading of the Word effective to save. Although the Bible contains everything we need to know for salvation, on its own, the bare Word will be ineffectual. We need the Holy Spirit to take the Word, and use it, and apply it for our salvation.

The other way of encountering the Word is through *"preaching."* Hearing the preached Word is the way in which most people come to know about Jesus and trust in Him. In fact, the Spirit *"especially"* makes the preached Word effective, more so than the read Word. The Catechism teaches us to expect greater blessing from hearing the Word preached than from reading the Word individually. When we gather in God's house to hear God's Word preached by God's ministers, we are putting ourselves in the best place to get maximum benefit from the Word. *"How shall they believe in him of whom they have not heard? And how shall they hear without a preacher?"* (Romans 10:14).

God has promised that when his Word is preached He is specially present by His Spirit to give an understanding of what is being said. When the preacher accurately and faithfully conveys the message of the Word of God to the minds, hearts, and conscience of the hearers, they are to accept it as coming with the same authority as the very Word of God itself. *"It pleased God by the foolishness of preaching to save them that believe"* (1 Corinthians 1:21).

Non-Christians need the Word of God

> "The Holy Spirit makes the Word effective for conversion."

The Holy Spirit makes the Word effective to salvation, both at the start of salvation, when a non-Christian becomes a Christian, and also throughout the Christian's career. If you are not a Christian, how do you need the Spirit to use the Word?

(a) The Word convinces the non-Christian

The Holy Spirit makes the Word effective for conviction. By the Word He convicts us of our sin and misery. He makes us convinced about it in the sense that we are persuaded beyond any possible doubt, we feel it something so completely proven that we are entirely defeated in argument. The Word defines and exposes sin. The Word explains the consequences of our sin. When the Spirit makes this effective, we don't just brush off this information as irrelevant, but instead realise that it means *I am a sinner and I need salvation from my sin.*

(b) The Word converts the non-Christian

The Holy Spirit makes the Word effective for conversion. Conversion is when the sinner is enabled to believe and repent for the very first time. The Word reveals Christ, who we are to believe in, and God, who we should repent towards. The Holy Spirit uses the Word to bring us to faith and repentance. He uses the Word the way someone might use a hammer to break a rock in pieces (Jeremiah 23:29), or the way someone uses a light to expose the secret wickedness of the heart (1 Corinthians 14:25; 2 Peter 1:19), or the way rain makes the earth bring forth and bud (Isaiah 55:10-11). For example, when Peter preached the Word in Jerusalem on the Day of Pentecost, the Word pricked his hearers in their hearts and prompted them to ask, *"Men and brethren, what shall we do?"* (Acts 2:37) and then they *"gladly received"* the Word (Acts 2:41).

Christians need the Word of God

(a) The Word of God **builds Christians up in holiness**

Once someone is converted, the Holy Spirit makes the Word effective for building them up. The Word builds us up in holiness by leading, correcting and rebuking us (2 Timothy 3:16-17). The Word also gives very clear and frequent revelations of the glory of Christ, in such a way that, by the working of the Spirit, the Christian grows in holiness and likeness to Jesus: *"But we all, with open face beholding as in a glass the glory of the Lord, are changed into the same image from glory to glory, even as by the Spirit of the Lord"* (2 Corinthians 3:18). In Ephesians 6, the Word of God is called *"the sword of the Spirit"* (verse 17). This sword is the only piece of attacking weaponry in the Christian's armour, and its cutting edge, and success against sin and Satan, comes from the Spirit who gave it.

(b) The Word of God **builds Christians up in comfort**

As Christians read the Word and hear it preached, they are reminded of the many promises of God for those who trust in Him. In their Bibles they read of their Saviour, the Lord Jesus, and all He has done for them. They see in their Bibles the lives of the people of God such as Abraham, David and Peter and what we they can learn from them. *"For whatsoever things were written aforetime were written for our learning, that we through patience and comfort of the scriptures might have hope"* (Romans 15:4).

(c) The Word of God is effective through faith

As the Holy Spirit makes the Word effectual, He uses an instrument - faith. The Word is effectual to salvation *"through faith."* If we don't believe what the Word says (about sin, Christ, holiness, or comfort) then it will do us no saving benefit. The Word of God is *"the power of God unto salvation to every one that believeth"* (Romans 1:16).

> "As Christians read the Word and hear it preached, they are reminded of the many promises of God for those who trust in Him."

🔍 Something to think about...

- Of all His ordinances, the preaching of the Word is the one which God has chosen to make especially effective for saving sinners. When you next hear a minister preaching, listen out to see which of the things he says are addressed to your mind, your heart (or emotions), and your conscience. How does the sermon aim to: **(a)** convince and convert you, and/or **(b)** build you up in holiness and comfort?

How can we get most from the Bible?

If it takes the Holy Spirit to make the Word effective to salvation, does this mean we have nothing to do? Far from it. Question 90 tells us how we must engage with the Word if it is going to be effectual to salvation.

90 How is the word to be read and heard, that it may become effectual to salvation?

A. That the word may become effectual to salvation, we must attend thereunto with diligence, preparation, and prayer; receive it with faith and love, lay it up in our hearts, and practise it in our lives.

Pay attention to the Word

The first thing we have to do with the Word is actually hear it. Whether we read it for ourselves or hear it preached, we have to **"attend thereunto"** - give it our attention. Three things should be features of our attending to the Word:

> "The first thing we have to do with the Word is actually hear it."

(a) Diligence
Diligence is the opposite of carelessness. We should be diligent about taking every opportunity to read the Word and hear it preached. We should be present at the Lord's day services regularly, not sporadically, and as frequently as our circumstances allow.

(b) Preparation
We should prepare our hearts to attend on the Word by reminding ourselves that it is in fact the Word of God, and that it is one of His ordinances for our salvation. We should also schedule our activities to help us prepare in practical ways: to avoid rushing in to church at the last minute, for example, or to prevent running out of time for personal Bible reading.

(c) Prayer
We should pray to the Lord that He would speak to us through the Word. We need to pray that we would be able to focus on His Word and not get distracted. We need to pray that the Holy Spirit would give us understanding, and open our hearts to the Word of God, as He did for Lydia (Acts 16:14). We can be confident that the Spirit who inspired the Word, will also give us help to understand the Word, in answer to prayer.

Accept the Word

How should we receive the Word of God when we are reading or hearing it?

(a) Faith

When we come to the Word of God we must believe that it is indeed God's Word, true and perfect in all it says, and the only authoritative guide we can have for all our spiritual needs. Faith should respond appropriately to the contents of the Word. When we encounter a threatening in the Word, our faith should tremble. When we encounter a promise in the Word, our faith should embrace it. When the Word is rightly preached, we should receive the message believingly, as having the same authority as the Scriptures themselves.

(b) Love

We are to receive the Word with love, because it is the Word of the God who is love and the God we love. The Word also reveals the most lovely truths and the beauty of holiness. The Psalmist couldn't stop talking about God's lovely Word. It was *"better unto me than thousands of gold and silver,"* and *"my delights." "I love [thy testimonies] exceedingly,"* he said (Psalm 119:72, 92, 167).

Keep the Word

(a) Lay it up in our hearts

In the parable of the sower, the birds came and stole away the seed and so nothing grew in the soil. The Lord says that is how Satan works, in order that we will not benefit from the Word. We have to guard against this by keeping the Word in our hearts. In Psalm 119 the psalmist says, *"Thy word have I hid in mine heart"* (verse 11). He kept it in his mind and often thought about it. It regulated his will and informed his conscience. It absorbed his affections and it stuck in his memory. If we hear the Word but do not keep it in our hearts, James says we deceive ourselves, and we are like a man who looks in the mirror but immediately forgets what he looks like.

> "We are not just to have the Word in our hearts; it always calls us to action and response."

(b) Put it into practice in our lives

We are not just to have the Word in our hearts; it always calls us to action and response. We are not only to be hearers of the Word but also doers (see James 1:22). If the Word, has a real lodging place in our hearts, it will inevitably show through as we put it into practice in our lives. The Word should be a lamp to our feet and a light to our path (Psalm 119:105). Our whole lifestyle and behaviour should be worthy of the gospel (Philippians 1:27).

🔍 Something to think about...

- Is there anything in the Word which we are to receive with faith but not with love? Is there anything in the Word which we are to receive with love but not with faith?

Personal reflection

Every time we encounter the Word (whether in private reading or public preaching), we should do so conscientiously, deliberately, and prayerfully. What things get in the way of you reading and hearing like this? What could you change so as to pay better attention to the Word?

God is able to bless His Word to save sinners even when they do not engage with it diligently. However, if you are half-hearted and careless in your attention to God's Word, this makes it obvious that you are not really interested in God's salvation for yourself. You say you want to be saved and go to heaven, but do you contradict yourself by the low level of attention you give to the Word?

How does grace come through the sacraments?

As well as the Word and prayer, God has also given us the sacraments as one of the main means by which Christ conveys to us the blessings of redemption. In the New Testament, there are two sacraments: baptism and the Lord's supper. Baptism is being washed with water to show forth union with Christ, while the Lord's supper is eating bread and drinking wine to show forth our dependence on the death of Christ. We will look at each of the sacraments in more detail shortly.

For now, Question 91 deals with the question of how we can benefit spiritually from the sacraments. Although we must be clear that the sacraments really are means of grace, there has been a lot of controversy in the Christian church down through the years, over what role exactly the sacraments play in communicating to us the benefits of redemption. In addressing this question, the Catechism steers us away from two things that are not true about the sacraments, followed by teaching us two things that are true about how the sacraments become effective means of grace.

> **91** How do the sacraments become effectual means of salvation?
>
> A. The sacraments become effectual means of salvation, not from any virtue in them, or in him that doth administer them; but only by the blessing of Christ, and the working of his Spirit in them that by faith receive them.

Two **great mistakes**

(a) The mistake of thinking that the sacraments have power in themselves

Some people believe that the very fact that you are baptised or take communion means that you have been spiritually blessed, no matter how your soul is, or how you live your life. But the sacraments have no *"virtue,"* or power, in themselves. They do not automatically or inevitably convey spiritual blessings. We can be baptised and not be a true child of God. Simon Magus was baptised but was later told by the Apostle Peter that his heart was *"not right in the sight of God"* (Acts 8:21). The same is true for the Lord's

> "We can sit at the Lord's supper and never be a Christian and at the end of our lives go to hell."

supper. We can sit at the Lord's supper, and never be a Christian, and at the end of our lives go to hell.

(b) The mistake of thinking that the sacraments have their power from the minister

We do not benefit from the sacrament because of any virtue or special power in *the person who is administering* the sacrament. The Roman Catholic Church believes that we benefit from the sacraments because of special power which the priest has. They teach that when the priest does his work properly, real spiritual help and blessing reach those taking part, and that unless the priest has the right intention when he administers the sacrament, no grace can be received by the participants. However, the Bible is very clear that, the minister who conducts the baptism or Lord's supper has no power to ensure that anyone receives real spiritual help and benefit from him. Nor does he have the ability to prevent people receiving a blessing even when he fails to do his work properly. *"Who then is Paul, and who is Apollos, but ministers by whom ye believed, even as the Lord gave to every man? I have planted, Apollos watered; but God gave the increase. So then neither is he that planteth any thing, neither he that watereth; but God that giveth the increase"* (1 Corinthians 3:5-7).

A lady once went to a communion service and heard the famous godly minister Ebenezer Erskine. She was greatly helped in her soul by the service that day and decided that in order to get the same blessing again she would go to the place where he was preaching the next Sabbath. She went to that place but did not get the same spiritual blessing. She was very disappointed and told Mr. Erskine. His reply was, *"Madam, the reason is this — last Sabbath you went to hear Jesus Christ; but today, you have come to hear Ebenezer Erskine."* We are looking for spiritual help in the wrong place if we expect it from the minister, instead of from Christ Himself.

Two great truths

(a) The sacraments are effective by the blessing of Christ

Instead of focussing on the human side of the sacraments (our participation or our minister's administration), we have to focus on the divine side to explain how the sacraments become effectual means of grace. The Catechism first mentions *"the blessing of Christ."* It is the Lord Jesus Christ who has appointed the sacraments as King and Head of His church. He set up the sacrament of the Lord's supper in Matthew 26:26-28 and He set up the sacrament of baptism in Matthew 28:19. Christ not only gave us the sacraments, but He also comes to our help in the sacraments, so that through the sacraments we really receive the blessings of salvation. In Matthew 18:20 the Lord speaks of those who gather in His name and gives the promise, *"There am I in the midst of them."*

> "It is the special work of the Holy Spirit to cleanse us from our sins in regeneration."

(b) The sacraments are effective by the work of the Holy Spirit

The sacraments become an effectual means of salvation when the Holy Spirit works through the sacraments and with the sacraments. It is the special work of the Holy Spirit to cleanse us from our sins in regeneration, and the special work of the Holy Spirit to enable us to feed on Christ and grow in grace. So, when we participate in the sacraments which display these benefits, we rely on the Holy Spirit to give us the reality which the sacraments signify.

The Catechism adds that the sacraments are effectual only to those people who receive them *"by faith."* By the faith which is the gift of the Spirit, we look beyond the symbols and ceremonies of the sacraments, and get the benefit of the spiritual things which the sacraments point to. Unbelievers do not get any saving benefit from participating in the sacraments.

🔍 Something to think about...

- Imagine that someone was baptised by a famous and well-respected minister. Later on, it transpires that the minister was cheating on his wife and embezzling money from church accounts at the time. Should this person now regard their baptism as worthless?
- Because the sacraments have no inherent power to convey grace to us, there is a risk of thinking that they are not particularly important for us to participate in. But the Catechism says that the sacraments are genuinely effectual means of grace. How does the thought of: (a) the blessing of Christ, and (b) the working of the Holy Spirit, help you to adjust your thoughts to valuing the sacraments appropriately?

What is a sacrament?

After clarifying the way in which we should view the sacraments as a means of grace, the Catechism now turns to some more specific points about the sacraments — how to define a sacrament, and the identity of the New Testament sacraments.

92 What is a sacrament?

A. A sacrament is a holy ordinance instituted by Christ, wherein, by sensible signs, Christ, and the benefits of the new covenant, are represented, sealed and applied to believers.

93 Which are the sacraments of the New Testament?

A. The sacraments of the New Testament are, Baptism and the Lord's supper.

Where did the sacraments come from?

"The sacraments can only be rightly administered by ordained ministers in Christ's church."

There are two sacraments in the New Testament: baptism and the Lord's supper. Why do we have these two, and only these two? Was it simply a case of some leading figures in the church long ago deciding that it would be a good idea to have them, and gradually this idea caught on until eventually it became the norm? Not at all. The Catechism reminds us that the sacraments were *"instituted"* or appointed *"by Christ."* Christ is the King and Head of the church, and He alone has the authority to appoint any of the church's ordinances, especially the sacraments.

In the Old Testament Christ gave His church circumcision (Genesis 17:9-14) and the passover (Exodus 12:1-14). Now in the New Testament He has given us baptism (Matthew 28:18-20) and the Lord's supper (Matthew 26:26-28).

Knowing that the sacraments came from Christ, it is also worth considering where we find the sacraments today.

* **Christ instituted His sacraments in His church.** It is never appropriate for individuals to go through the motions of administering either baptism or the Lord's supper in their own homes, or in any context other than the formal, corporate church of Christ. The sacraments can only be rightly administered by ordained ministers in Christ's church. They are public services, not private, personal devotions.

- **Christ instituted His sacraments alongside His Word.** We wouldn't know what the signs and actions in a sacrament meant if it wasn't for the Word. We wouldn't even know what sacraments existed if it wasn't for the Word. We rely on the Word (read and preached) for our right to observe the sacraments, for the right way of observing the sacraments, for interpreting to us what the sacraments mean, and for explaining to us what blessings we are to expect from participating in them.

What role do the sacraments perform?

Question 92 tells us that the whole point of the sacraments is *"Christ and the benefits of the new covenant."* This is another way of saying the person and work of Christ. Our focus in the sacraments should be on Christ the Saviour and the blessings He gives sinners, whether justification, sanctification, adoption, or any of the benefits which accompany or flow from these.

The connection between the sacraments, and Christ and His benefits, is that the sacraments *represent, seal, and apply* them.

- The water in baptism, and the bread and wine in the supper, *represent* or portray something about Christ and His benefits. They picture for us the need to be saved, the only way in which we can be saved, and how to go on in the way of salvation. In baptism there is a resemblance between water and spiritual cleansing by the Spirit. In the Lord's supper there is a resemblance between bread and wine, and spiritual feeding on Christ's body and blood.
- The sacraments *seal* Christ and His benefits to the believer. A seal authenticates, confirms, and guarantees that something is genuine. For example, the orb mark on tweed is a seal to guarantee that with piece of tweed is genuine Harris Tweed. The sacraments guarantee to believers that Christ and His benefits really do belong to them. They are pledges that God really will fulfil all the promises He makes in the new covenant.
- The sacraments *apply* Christ and His benefits to the believer. They actually communicate, or convey, or administer Christ and His benefits in a spiritual way.

How do the sacraments perform this role?

In the sacraments, Christ and His benefits are represented, sealed, and applied *"by sensible signs."*

The signs
- The signs are the sacramental *elements,* which are used in the sacramental actions. In baptism, the sacramental element is water, and it is used in the sacramental action of washing in the name of the Trinity. In the Lord's supper, the elements are bread and wine, and they are used in the sacramental actions of giving and receiving the bread and wine.
- The signs in a sacrament *signify* something. They point away from themselves to something else, to spiritual realities (namely, Christ and His benefits).

The senses

- ***The signs in a sacrament are intended to be perceived through the senses.*** They are *sense-able* signs. In both the sacraments we use the sense of sight, as we watch what happens with the water, and the bread and wine. In baptism we also use the sense of touch as we feel the water, and in the Lord's supper we use the sense of taste as we eat the bread and drink the wine.

> "The sacrament is addressed not only to our ears, but also to all our senses."

- ***A sacrament is designed to do exactly the same thing as a sermon but in a different way.*** The sermon is addressed to our ears; we listen, hear and learn. The sacrament is addressed not only to our ears, but also to all our senses. The sacraments are a kind of visible sermon. In fact the sacraments are the only pictures and images of Christ we are allowed to use, the ones the Lord Himself has given to us.

🔍 Something to think about...

- After the Flood, God told Noah that He would put the rainbow in the sky as His pledge that He would remember His covenant, and that the world would not be destroyed by a flood again. However, the rainbow has no power to prevent a flood. What then is the use of the rainbow? How does this help you understand the use of the sacraments?

- You can't get the benefit of Christ and His saving work from a sacrament unless you are a believer. How does this make the sacraments different from the reading and preaching of the Word as a means of grace?

- In John Bunyan's allegory, *The Holy War,* the metaphor of a town is used to represent the human soul. The town of Mansoul has five gates: Ear Gate, Eye Gate, Mouth Gate, Nose Gate, and Feel Gate, and nothing can get into the town through these gates except by permission from the townspeople inside. Can you think of what sort of things get in through each gate when the townspeople give permission for sinful things? Once the town gives its allegiance to Christ, different things get permission to come in. What sort of things get into the soul by these gates when the Christian participates in the sacraments?

What is baptism?

Having seen from Question 93 that there are two sacraments, we come now to consider in greater detail the first of these, the sacrament of baptism. The essence of baptism is that the person being baptised is washed with water in the name of the Father, and of the Son, and of the Holy Spirit.

> **94** What is baptism?
>
> A. Baptism is a sacrament, wherein the washing with water in the name of the Father, and of the Son, and of the Holy Ghost, doth signify and seal our ingrafting into Christ, and partaking of the benefits of the covenant of grace, and our engagement to be the Lord's.

A washing **and a name**

When someone is baptised, they are *washed with water.* Washing the body with water reminds us of our need of spiritual cleansing from the guilt and defilement of sin. The Bible talks about being spiritually cleansed both by the blood of Christ, and also by the washing of the Spirit. The blood of Christ is the basis for us being cleansed from the guilt of sin in justification, while the washing of the Spirit is what brings about our cleansing from the defilement of sin in regeneration and sanctification.

When this washing is done *"in the name of the Father, and of the Son, and of the Holy Ghost,"* it reminds us that all three persons of the Godhead are involved in the salvation of any sinner. The Father loved them, the Son redeemed them, and the Holy Spirit applies redemption to them. It emphasizes that the authority of the Triune God is behind the sacrament of baptism. It should also remind us that when we

> "The blood of Christ is the basis for us being cleansed from the guilt of sin in justification."

are baptised, we are being identified with the one living and true God, and with His people.

The Catechism says that washing with water in the name of the Trinity *"doth signify and seal"* something. It *signifies* by pointing away from itself to a greater spiritual reality. The water itself is not the spiritual blessing, but it is a sign of the spiritual blessing. It *seals* by confirming the truthfulness of what God promises. Of course, God's promise is already as truthful and as certain as it is possible to be. But God kindly makes allowances for the weakness of our faith, by giving extra forms of confirmation over and above the promise itself.

Union with Christ

The core meaning of baptism is union with Christ. The Catechism refers to this as *"ingrafting into Christ."* This borrows the idea of grafting one plant into another in horticulture. When you graft a twig onto a tree, it makes a join so that the twig then takes its life and growth from the tree. Christ calls Himself a vine, and His people are the branches (John 15). When someone is united to Christ, that person then relies entirely on Christ for their spiritual life and spiritual growth.

Participating in covenant blessings

Once someone is united to Christ, they partake *"of the benefits of the covenant of grace."* Baptism focusses our minds particularly on benefits such as:

- Pardon of sins by the blood of Christ (Acts 2:38)
- Regeneration by the Spirit (Titus 3:5)
- Adoption into God's family (Galatians 3:26-27), including the family of His disciples in the church on earth (Matthew 28:19)
- Resurrection to everlasting life (Romans 6:3-5). The believer who is united to Christ participates both in His death and in His resurrection life.

Belonging to the Lord

When a man and a woman get engaged to be married, they make a wholehearted commitment to each other. Baptism is a sign and seal of *"our engagement to be the Lord's."*

> "We no longer belong to ourselves, and we also completely disown any claim that the world or Satan might make on us."

On our side, this means we make the wholehearted commitment that we belong to God the Father, Son, and Holy Spirit. We will belong wholly and only to the Lord, body and soul, along with all that we have, whether gifts or graces or possessions. We no longer belong to ourselves, and we also completely disown any claim that the world or Satan might make on us. This is the promise made in baptism. Where children are baptised they are under an obligation to fulfill these promises as they grow up and be only and wholly the Lord's.

On the Lord's side, this means that Father, Son, and Holy Spirit commit themselves wholeheartedly to be our God, to save us and keep us and bless us. God promises that He *"will be their God, and they shall be my people"* (Jeremiah 31:33).

🔍 Something to think about...

- What two kinds of washing does baptism signify?
- Why is it important for people to be baptised in the name of the Father, and of the Son, and of the Holy Ghost?

Personal reflection

Although baptism is only meant to be administered once, it should give shape and character to the whole subsequent life of the baptised person. If you have been baptised, how does your life testify to the blessedness of union with Christ, participation in covenant blessings, and belonging to the Lord?

Who should be baptised?

Question 94 has given a definition of the sacrament of baptism. Now Question 95 tackles the question of who should be baptised.

> **95** To whom is baptism to be administered?
>
> A. Baptism is not to be administered to any that are out of the visible church, till they profess their faith in Christ, and obedience to him; but the infants of such as are members of the visible church are to be baptized.

Baptism is **strictly limited**

Visible and invisible

The one church of Christ can be considered in two ways. One way is to focus on those who are actually saved, the whole number of the elect in all times and places. Only God knows for sure who each of these people are. They are not known with completeness or certainty to other people. The term used to refer to the church considered this way is *'the invisible church.'*

The other way to consider the church of Christ is as people align themselves formally and publicly to the Christian religion. They are not atheists or followers of a false religion, and are associated with Christianity. The term **"visible church"** is used to refer to all those who belong to the Christian faith in this outward way. Some, but not all the people who belong to the visible church, are actually saved. Nevertheless, they belong to a special group who enjoy special privileges. They belong to the community whom God takes special care of; they enjoy the friendship, support, and encouragement of other Christians; and they benefit from the preaching of the Word, public prayer, and pastoral care. These advantages belong to everyone in the visible church, whether or

"To profess obedience to Christ is to live your life consistent with God's commandments."

not they have the union and communion with Christ, which is enjoyed by the members of the invisible church.

It is not right to give baptism to just anyone and everyone who asks for it. Only those who belong to the visible church are to receive baptism.

Faith and obedience

Baptism is reserved for those who profess their faith in Christ and their willingness to be obedient to Him. To **"profess faith in Christ"** is to acknowledge Him as the only Saviour of sinners. Anyone who is not willing to acknowledge this is disqualified from receiving baptism. To **"profess ... obedience to Christ"** is to live your life consistent with God's commandments, and to commit to doing so from now on. Anyone who is not prepared to obey Christ is disqualified from receiving baptism.

If someone approaches the church seeking baptism, and on being questioned says that they believe that there are many ways to heaven and that we do not necessarily have to believe in Jesus, then it would be wrong to baptise them. Again, if someone wishing baptism has a grasp of Christian doctrine but shows that they have no intention of ever obeying the commands of God, it would not be right to grant them baptism. Someone seeking baptism, but not willing to attend church on a regular basis, or notorious in the community for taking God's name in vain, for example, is quite clearly not willing to have their life ruled by the Word of God, and has no right to be baptised.

Baptism is **wonderfully inclusive**

Baptism is for everyone who is in the visible church. There are two ways of being in the visible church.

Members by **profession**

One way is for someone who previously rejected Christianity to now profess their faith in Christ, and their obedience to Him. This is what happens when atheists and followers of false religions come to hear the Word of God, and to realise that Jesus is the only Saviour. Once they commit themselves to believing His truth and following His commandments, then they place themselves inside the visible church, and it is appropriate to baptise them. In Acts 8 we read of two people being baptised. One was the Ethiopian eunuch. As soon as he acknowledged that Jesus Christ was the Son of God, he was baptised. The other was Simon Magus. He believed Philip when he preached about the kingdom of God and the name of Jesus Christ. Both these baptisms were appropriate, even though Simon Magus shortly afterwards showed in a shocking way, that he had no real appreciation of who the Holy Spirit was or how He worked.

> "The baby children of people who belong to the visible church, also belong to it, and therefore, it is appropriate to baptise them."

Members by **birth**

The other way of being in the visible church is when you are born into it. The baby children of people who belong to the visible church, also belong to it, and therefore, it is appropriate to baptise them. Therefore it is appropriate to baptise them. This is similar to the situation where, if you are born in the UK to UK parents, you are automatically a UK citizen and entitled to a UK passport. God established this principle in the Old Testament, when He made a covenant with Abraham which included Abraham's children who were not even then born. *"And I will establish my covenant between me and thee and thy seed after thee in their generations for an everlasting covenant, to be a God unto thee, and to thy seed after thee"* (Genesis 17:7). On this basis these children were given what was then the sign of the covenant, circumcision. God continues this principle in the New Testament. God has not said that in the New Testament children are no longer to be included as belonging to the covenant community. In Acts 2:39 the apostle Peter assures his hearers that *"the promise is unto you, and to your children."* In 1 Corinthians 7:14 the apostle Paul explains that if even one parent is a Christian, then the child is to be viewed as belonging to the visible church.

🔍 Something to think about...

- For what reasons would it be appropriate for the church to refuse to baptise somebody?
- Is it right to ask people to prove that they are born again before they can be baptised?

How does grace come through the Lord's supper?

Having considered the sacrament of baptism we now turn to the second of the two New Testament sacraments, the Lord's supper.

96 What is the Lord's supper?

A. The Lord's supper is a sacrament, wherein by giving and receiving bread and wine, according to Christ's appointment, his death is showed forth; and the worthy receivers are, not after a corporal and carnal manner, but by faith, made partakers of his body and blood, with all his benefits, to their spiritual nourishment and growth in grace.

What is done in the Lord's supper?

> "The giving of the bread and wine points to God giving Christ, and Christ giving Himself for His people and to His people."

Giving and receiving

In the Lord's supper, bread and wine are given and received. The bread and wine point to the death of Christ (His broken body and shed blood) on behalf of His people, when He satisfied divine justice and reconciled them to God. The giving of the bread and wine points to God giving Christ, and Christ giving Himself for His people and to His people. The receiving of the bread and wine points to the believer taking Christ to their soul in faith and love for their spiritual life, survival and health.

As Christ has appointed

The giving and receiving of bread and wine is done *"according to Christ's appointment"*.

- We do it because the Lord Himself has told us to do it. The night before He died on the cross, the Lord Jesus held the first communion service with His disciples. He told them about His sufferings and death which were shortly to take place, and He told them that this special service was not just a one-off event never to be done again, but something to be repeated by the church over and over again until His second coming at the end of time.
- We also do it in the way in which Christ has appointed it. In 1 Corinthians 11:23-26 the Apostle Paul gives the church more details as to how this service should be conducted. The minister takes the bread and the cup of wine, gives thanks, breaks the bread, and gives the bread and the wine to the communicants. The communicants take the bread and the cup, and eat the bread and drink the wine.

What does the Lord's supper do?

> "In the Lord's supper the people of God remember what their Saviour did for them when He suffered and died in their place."

In the giving and receiving of bread and wine in this sacrament *"Christ's ... death is showed forth,"* or portrayed, or displayed. The broken bread is a symbol of the body of our Lord Jesus, which was so cruelly broken in His sufferings before and during His crucifixion. The poured out wine symbolises the Lord's blood, which He shed for the remission of sins.

How is the death of Christ *"showed forth"* in the Lord's supper?

- **It reminds us** of the fact that Christ died. In the Lord's supper the people of God remember what their Christ did for them when He suffered and died in their place. The Lord's supper is an ongoing reminder, a continuing memorial, of the work and sufferings of Christ. The Lord told the disciples, *"This do in remembrance of me"* (Luke 22:19). It is not in any way an attempt to recreate what He did on the cross but it does recall what happened.

- **It displays** the meaning of Christ's death. He did not die as the helpless victim of the oppressive Roman authorities, nor merely as an example of how much can be patiently suffered in a good cause. Christ's death was a substitutionary atonement. He acted on behalf of all and only His elect people. He atoned for sin, putting away the guilt of sin, and turning away the wrath of God.

- **It testifies** to the success of Christ's death. Believers will continue to partake of the Lord's supper until Christ comes again. When they look forward to Him coming again, it shows that they believe He is alive and reigning now, as a consequence of the fact that His death achieved its intended purpose. He is now making continual intercession for them, and He is unfolding all of providence for their good. It also means that they live their lives expecting and anticipating His second coming, when He will judge the world in righteousness, and finally send the wicked to hell and bring His people to heaven to be with Himself.

- **It proclaims** that Christ's death and its meaning and consequences matter to us. Those who sit at the Lord's supper witness by their actions that they rely on Christ for everything. Instead of being ashamed of the cross of Christ, communicants tell to all around that this is the power of God and the wisdom of God, and they are pleased that this is the case. His death is the only basis they have for their hope of salvation, and their life and wellbeing depends entirely on being fed and supported by Christ.

How do we benefit from the Lord's supper?

By partaking

Those who sit at the Lord's supper are *"made partakers of [Christ's] body and blood, with all his benefits."* They partake of Christ Himself: His righteousness, His love, His atonement, His forgiveness, and His fellowship. We can understand this partaking in the sense of feeding. Food in the cupboard, or food on the plate, does us no good unless we actually eat it. So the death of Christ and the blessings He purchased by it, will do us no good unless we actually take them into our souls. Our souls have to eat Christ's flesh spiritually and drink His blood spiritually (John 6:53-56). This is eating and drinking is done by our souls in the sacrament as we eat and drink the bread and the wine.

By faith

Some people wrongly think that they will automatically be blessed just by taking part in the Lord's supper, but in reality we benefit from it only *"by faith."* Only those who trust the Saviour are going to receive any benefit from sitting at the Lord's supper. Faith enables the believer to look beyond the physical signs of the bread and wine to the spiritual realities which they signify. Faith enables the believer to take hold of these spiritual realities and receive them in their souls. Although unbelievers may consume the bread and wine, nobody can partake of the body and blood of Christ in any sense if they do not have faith.

Those who sit at the Lord's supper are made partakers of the body and blood of Christ by faith, and *"not after a corporal and carnal manner"* (that is, not in a physical and bodily way). This counteracts one of the errors of the Roman Catholic Church, namely the claim that the bread and the wine are changed into the literal body and blood of Christ, so that Christ is physically present in the sacrament.

We do not believe that Christ is *physically* present in the Lord's supper. The bread and wine remain bread and wine. However, we do believe that Christ is *spiritually* present in the Lord's supper. The realities about the person and work of Christ, which are signified by the bread and wine, are partaken of by the soul, as they are received by faith, and through the power of the Holy Spirit.

> "Pardon and sanctification are things which all the Lord's people have in common."

By feeding spiritually

We eat our food not simply as fuel, but also with enjoyment. Bread is not just a staple foodstuff, but is also tasty; and wine is refreshing and cheering. So the blessings of Christ's death are not only to grant us mere life and survival, but we are to enjoy the taste of pardon, and delight in the sense of His love.

The best meals are part of a social occasion in the good company of our friends and loved ones. There is a shared, communal aspect to the partaking involved in the Lord's supper. The blessings of Christ's death are not only individualistic, private gifts but things shared with others. Pardon and sanctification are things which all the Lord's people have in common. At the Lord's supper, each one sits down in the company of others, and they all (each and together) have communion with Christ in His death and the blessings He gives them. As they sit together at the Lord's supper, Christians are reminded of the unity there

> "Christ and His benefits keep the soul healthy and active in the ways of God."

is between the people of God who have been adopted into the one family. The Lord's supper is also a way for Christians to identify themselves in a public and committed way with the people of God. By sitting at the Lord's supper with the people of God, a person is saying that they are a Christian who trusts in the Lord Jesus Christ as their Lord and Saviour.

When we eat good food, it does us good. It gives us strength and energy for our daily work, and it keeps us healthy. Christ and His benefits keep the soul healthy and active in the ways of God. Christians sitting at the Lord's supper are encouraged to remember that though they are poor sinners, they have a great Saviour who loved them and died in their place. The Lord's supper also reminds them of their privileges and responsibilities as the covenant people of God. The Lord's supper is also an encouragement to the believer in the struggle with sin and Satan. It is as if the Lord is saying in the sacrament, *'Look at what I have done for you; now you go on walking faithfully with me.'*

Q Something to think about...

- In what ways are bread and wine appropriate symbols for representing nourishment by the body and blood of Christ?

Personal reflection

If you sit at the Lord's supper, you are *'showing forth'* (displaying or testifying) certain things. If you do not sit at the Lord's supper, you are testifying that you reject and contradict those same things. Does your outward behaviour in participating or not participating in the Lord's supper match the inward desires of your heart?

How do we take the Lord's supper in a worthy manner?

According to Question 96, it is only "worthy receivers" who actually partake of Christ and His benefits in this sacrament. Question 97 now explains what is meant by "worthy receiving."

💬 What is required to the worthy receiving of the Lord's supper?

A. It is required of them that would worthily partake of the Lord's supper that they examine themselves of their knowledge to discern the Lord's body, of their faith to feed upon him, of their repentance, love, and new obedience; lest, coming unworthily, they eat and drink judgment to themselves.

Partaking worthily **is a serious activity**

> "Faith is ... a prerequisite for sitting at the Lord's supper."

To sit at the Lord's supper is a very serious thing. There is a difference between those that would *"worthily partake"* and those *"coming unworthily."* This terminology echoes what we find in the New Testament passages which deal with this sacrament (especially 1 Corinthians 11:27-29). Faith is, of course, a prerequisite for sitting at the Lord's supper. Nobody is qualified to sit at the Lord's supper if they do not have faith. Yet even believers have to consider whether they are coming worthily or unworthily.

This is not a question of *deserving* to sit at the Lord's supper. Nobody deserves to come to the Lord's supper, or indeed to receive anything else from God. Rather than looking at whether *the person* is *"worthy,"* we have to focus on whether their coming and their partaking is done *"worthily."* According to 1 Corinthians 11:28, when a person comes to the Lord's supper and partakes of the supper they should do it in a way of self-examination: *"Let a man examine himself, and so [i.e., in this manner] let him eat of that bread and drink of that cup."*

We should also note that the church has its own serious responsibility to make sure that this sacrament is treated with the reverence that is appropriate for the things of God. This is why, in our practice, people are examined by the minister and elders before they come to the Lord's supper for the first time. It is also why we *'fence'* the table every time the Lord's supper is administered: when the minister makes clear from the Bible who are invited to the Lord's supper and who ought not to go to it.

Partaking worthily **requires a searching examination**

We must take care not to give the impression that no one can ever come to the Lord's supper. The Lord calls His own people to the table, and, ideally, all the Lord's people would take their place at the table. However, no one should come to the Lord's supper without examining themselves. This means investigating themselves in a detailed and honest way, in the light of God's Word, accompanied with prayer for the help of God's Spirit. The Catechism sets out for us the main areas of examination.

Knowledge to discern the Lord's body

We are to examine ourselves to see if we understand what we are doing. Do we appreciate the difference between the death of Christ and every other death? Do we understand that the bread in the sacrament points away from itself to the body of Christ? Do we have more than head knowledge of the

> "We are to examine ourselves to see if we understand what we are doing."

way of salvation? Do we just know about Christ as Saviour because we have heard He is a Saviour, or do we know Him as our Saviour in a personal way?

Faith to feed on Christ

We have to examine ourselves to see if we have faith to feed on Christ. Do we have the faith which receives and rests on Christ alone for salvation? Do we find all our spiritual hunger satisfied in Christ? Is He our Redeemer? Do we have the faith which receives into our souls all the spiritual food which the bread and wine symbolise? *"Examine yourselves, whether ye be in the faith"* (2 Corinthians 13:5).

Repentance, love, and new obedience

- Are we penitent? David says, *"...I will declare mine iniquity; I will be sorry for my sin"* (Psalm 38:18). Are we, like David, confessing our iniquity, grieving over our sin, and turning from it with grief and hatred? Or are we harbouring sin in our heart? If we have fallen into open and disgraceful sin, even if we are true believers, it would not be appropriate for us to be permitted to sit at the Lord's supper until we repent.
- Are we loving? Do we love the Lord? Do we love our fellow believers, especially those who will sit at the same table as us? Do we love our neighbours in general? Is there evidence of love for the Lord and the things of God (His Word, His day, His people) in our lives?
- Are we obedient? The concept of *"new obedience"* has already been mentioned in Question 87. Referring back to that question, do we make the constant, serious effort to live a righteous life? Do we obey the Lord out of love, because of the love of Christ, whole-heartedly, and for the glory of God?

What if examination shows we come short?

If our self-examination reveals that we do not have faith at all, then we must not go to the Lord's supper. Instead we must believe and repent. Unconverted people who do not know, trust, love or obey the Lord have no right to sit at His table. If they do so, they will bring temporal, spiritual and perhaps eternal judgment on themselves (1 Corinthians 11:29);

> "No true Christian has ever found sufficient love, faith or obedience in their own heart."

they *"eat and drink judgement to themselves."* If our self-examination reveals that we do have faith, but only a little faith and a little grace, then we should not necessarily exclude ourselves from the Lord's supper. The truth is that every Christian will be dissatisfied with what they find when they examine themselves. No true Christian has ever found sufficient love, faith or obedience in their own heart. The Apostle Paul said, *"O wretched man that I am!"* (Romans 7:24). However, the Lord's supper is intended to be a means for faith and all the graces to be fed and strengthened. If a believer is conscious of their need of forgiveness and cleansing, and of the Lord's help to live more consistently, then there is a good match between their condition and the purpose of this sacrament. Even when a believer is full of fears and doubts, they can come to the Lord's supper with the expectation that the Lord will bless it by enabling them to partake of Christ and His benefits for their spiritual nourishment and growth in grace.

🔍 Something to think about...

Using the criteria in **Question 97**, explain whether each of the following people would come worthily to the Lord's supper.

- **Person A** is resolved to lead a holy life, and shows her love to her neighbour by working for a charity in a deprived inner city area. She loves the Lord and worships Him as He is physically present in the bread and wine.
- **Person B** was converted in his early twenties under a well-known orthodox minister. He is widely respected for his gentleness and his grasp of the Reformed faith. At a social reception he recently had to attend for work, he disgraced himself by drinking too much and had to be taken home in a taxi. The minister and elders have not yet had the opportunity to meet him to discuss the situation.
- **Person C** has struggled for a long time to discern whether she genuinely grieves over her sin, or whether her circumspect lifestyle is just the product of her upbringing in a godly home. Her thoughts turn constantly to the astonishing love of Christ when He died on the cross for sinners, and she longs to have Him for her own Saviour.

What is prayer?

Back in Question 85, we saw that God makes several requirements of us, in order for us to escape His wrath and curse due to us for sin. We have already looked at faith and repentance (Questions 86 and 87). We have also covered two of the three special means of grace, the Word (Questions 89 and 90) and the sacraments (Questions 91 to 97). Now, Question 98 opens the final section of the Catechism. From now to the end of the Catechism, we are looking at prayer, the third of the three special means of grace.

💬 What is prayer?

A. Prayer is an offering up of our desires unto God, for things agreeable to his will, in the name of Christ, with confession of our sins, and thankful acknowledgement of his mercies.

Who are we to pray to?

Prayer is *"an offering up of our desires unto God."* It is presenting Him with our wishes. When Psalm 62 tells us to pray, it says, *"Pour out your heart before him"* (verse 8).

Prayer is a part of religious worship
It is therefore to be offered only to God. He alone is able to hear and answer our prayers. God is our Creator, and we are dependent on Him for our existence. God is the God of providence, and we are dependent on Him to supply all the needs we have in this life. God is also the God of salvation. We are totally dependent on Him if we are to escape His wrath and curse due to us for sin, and receive the benefits of Christ's redemption.

Some people believe that they can also pray to those who have died, such as the apostles or other famous people who they regard as saints. Nowhere in the Bible are we encouraged to pray to people who have died. Instead the Bible teaches us that saints, no matter who they are, are unable to hear or help us. Prayer is to be directed only to the Lord.

> "God is our Creator, and we are dependent on Him for our existence."

How are we to pray?

In the name of Christ
Praying *"in the name of Christ"* means asking for mercy for His sake, not for our sake. This is more than simply ending our prayers with a form of words such as, *'For Jesus' sake, Amen.'* It means praying in obedience to Christ's command to pray. It means having confidence in Christ's promises when we pray. It means drawing our encouragement to pray from Christ and His mediation. It means finding in Christ and His mediation all the boldness we need, all the strength we need, and all our hope of being accepted, when we approach God in prayer.

With confession
As we come in prayer we must come *"with confession of our sins"* and our utter unworthiness to receive anything from the Lord.

Our confession is to be full and free, with grief and hatred for our failure and wrongdoing in thought, word and deed. Daniel shows such an attitude when he says, *"We have sinned, and have committed iniquity, and have done wickedly, and have rebelled... O Lord, righteousness belongeth unto thee, but unto us confusion of faces"* (Daniel 9:5&7). Our confession should be accompanied by a humble attitude, as demonstrated by the publican, who was so full of shame that he *"would not lift up so much as his eyes unto heaven"* (Luke 18:13). We are assured in Psalm 10:17 that while the Lord rejects the proud, He hears the desire of the humble.

With thanksgiving

Every good thing we receive from the Lord deserves our thanks. This includes the good things of this life, and it is especially true of His great mercy towards sinners. In speaking to the Philippians, the apostle joined thankfulness and prayer as inseparably connected, *"By prayer and supplication with thanksgiving let your requests be made known unto God"* (Philippians 4:6).

By the Spirit's help

Although the Shorter Catechism does not say so explicitly, we must also pray with the help of the Holy Spirit. We are too spiritually ignorant and too spiritually infirm to pray as we should. We need the Holy Spirit to teach us what to pray for and to strengthen us to pray with earnestness, zeal and focus instead of superficially, half-heartedly, and with wandering thoughts. *"Likewise the Spirit also helpeth our infirmities: for we know not what we should pray for as we ought"* (Romans 8:26).

What are we to pray for?

We are to pray *"for things agreeable to His will."* It is easy to ask for things that are agreeable to our will. But in prayer we should ask only for things that are in harmony with what God wishes, even if sometimes it goes against our own will. The way we know what things are in accordance with God's will is by referring to His Word. Here are some examples:

> "We are too spiritually ignorant and too spiritually infirm to pray as we should."

- **Spiritual blessings.** We should pray for pardon, spiritual life and help and strength, deliverance from evil, the advancement of Christ's kingdom and everything that glorifies God.
- **Providential blessings.** We should seek from the Lord whatever blessings connected to this life we stand in need of.
- **Many People.** We should pray for providential, and especially for spiritual blessings, for our family and friends, colleagues and neighbours, fellow Christians, our minister and elders, the whole Christian church, those in authority, those in need, and our enemies.
- **Lawful things.** We must not pray for things that are sinful. We must not pray for a blessing on things that are morally wrong.
- **Living people.** We are not to pray for people who have died, or for anyone who is known to have sinned the sin unto death.

🔍 Something to think about...

Personal reflection

We have always to beware of thinking that if we just repeat words, we have prayed. God is not interested in long or fine-sounding prayers, but in the real desires of our hearts. If you were to put into words the deepest longing of your heart, would it be for something agreeable to God's will?

We also need to beware of knowing what prayer is, but never actually praying. As a dependent creature with many needs and unmet desires, do you present your needs to God who is able to meet all our needs and more? As a rebellious creature with many iniquities to be pardoned, do you ever make use of Christ as your mediator to approach and be reconciled to God? As a saved sinner in constant need of sanctifying, do you constantly appeal to the Lord to preserve you and help you to grow in holiness?

How should we pray?

Question 98 gave us a definition of prayer. But God is so holy, so wonderful and so powerful. How is it best to pray to Him? We are advised in Ecclesiastes 5:2, "Be not rash with thy mouth, and let not thine heart be hasty to utter anything before God: for God is in heaven, and thou upon earth: therefore let thy words be few." But how do we know how to express ourselves appropriately and concisely? Here the Catechism speaks of two guides we have for prayer, and we will look at each in turn.

> **99** What rule hath God given for our direction in prayer?
>
> A. The whole Word of God is of use to direct us in prayer; but the special rule of direction is that form of prayer which Christ taught His disciples, commonly called The Lord's prayer.

General guide to prayer

If we are looking for guidance on how to pray, we can make use of *"the whole Word of God."* Throughout the Bible we can find useful guidance and direction in prayer. In what ways can the Bible as a whole help us in prayer?

"The whole Word of God is of use to direct us in prayer."

(a) It provides us with **instruction to pray**
The Bible contains the direct instruction to pray. *"Take with you words, and turn to the LORD: say unto him, Take away all iniquity, and receive us graciously..."* (Hosea 14:2). Whatever our spiritual condition is, and however sinful and deficient our prayers may be, the Bible instructs us to turn to God. If we are not saved, we must pray for salvation; and we make our situation worse by refusing to pray. If we are saved, we have liberty to approach God as our loving Father.

(b) It provides us with **examples of prayer**
The Bible is full of examples to guide us. We have examples of short prayers. In Genesis we have the prayers of Abraham and Jacob. Later on we have the prayers of Nehemiah and Elijah. The Book of Psalms contains many short prayers. In the New Testament we have the prayers of our Lord and of the Apostles. In the Gospel of Luke we find the prayer of the publican, *"God be merciful to me a sinner"* (18:13). We also have examples of longer prayers. These include the prayer of Solomon at the dedication of the temple (2 Chronicles 6), Daniel's prayer of confession (Daniel 9), Nehemiah's prayer for help (Nehemiah 1:4-11), Paul's desire for his fellow believers (Ephesians 3:14-21), and the intercessory prayer of Christ (John 17). Long or short, they are there to be read and learned from.

"The Bible instructs us to turn to God."

(c) It provides us with **the manner of prayer**

We are to pray with humility. *"Wherewith shall I come before the Lord, and bow myself before the high God?"* (Micah 6:6). We are to pray with understanding (1 Corinthians 14:15). We are to pray with persistence. *"I will not let thee go, except thou bless me"* (Genesis 32:26). We are to pray with expectation. *"I early will direct / my prayer to thee, and looking up, / an answer will expect"* (Psalm 5:3 metrical).

(d) It provides us with **themes for prayer**

All the themes of Scripture can be turned into prayer. When the Bible tells us truths about who God is, we can pray for Him to be known and worshipped accordingly. When it tells us what God has promised to do, we can pray for Him to do these things. When it tells us how God has punished sin and helped His people, we can pray for Him to help us avoid those same sins, and to make us thankful for His kindnesses. The whole Word of God is full of things we can use as prompts either to ask for something, confess something, or give thanks for something.

Special guide to prayer

Not only do we have a general guide to prayer but we also have a special guide, usually known as *"the Lord's prayer."* This is found in Matthew 6:9-13 (and in a slightly different form in Luke 11:2-4). In what ways is the Lord's prayer a special guide for us?

a) It gives us **teaching about prayer**

This is the prayer which Christ responded with when the disciples specifically asked Him, *"Lord, teach us to pray"* (Luke 11:1). He introduced it by saying that they should pray *"after this manner"* (Matthew 6:9).

(b) It gives us **themes for prayer**

It brings together, in a few short sentences, the major themes we find elsewhere in the Bible. It is a God-centred prayer: it begins and ends with God, His person, power and glory, and seeks the advance of God's kingdom. It contains confession of sin and a plea for pardon. It seeks help and blessing for our bodies and souls, and also those of others.

(c) It gives us **encouragement for prayer**

The brief and simple nature of the Lord's prayer encourages us to understand that prayer is not just for very clever and learned or spiritual people. We can all understand, follow and learn from this guide. It contains nothing that is inappropriate for anyone to ask, whether they are saved or unsaved.

(d) It gives us **a template for prayer**

If we are stuck for how to express ourselves in prayer, we can turn to the exact words of the Lord's prayer. We know that it is right to pray for these things, in these terms, because the Lord specifically sets this out for us. Nevertheless, we are not limited to these exact words. The Lord did not intend the disciples to stick rigidly to only those exact words, as we can see from the fact that there are two different versions of this same prayer (Matthew 6 and Luke 11). There are various examples of the apostles and other believers praying in the Acts and Epistles which ask for different things in different ways, and address God in different ways.

Nor does it mean that we are required to repeat these exact words in prayer regularly. Some churches repeat this prayer regularly in their services.

We believe that such a practice misunderstands the purpose of the Lord's prayer as a general template for prayer rather than an exact form of words which must obligatorily be repeated day by day or week by week. Prayer is to come first and foremost, not from our head but from our heart. Whether we use the form of the Lord's prayer or some other form of words, it is not simply to be a parrot-like repetition of certain words but a real reflection of our thoughts and needs. Even if we find ourselves repeatedly using the same phrases to express our recurring needs, we must beware of doing this in a *"vain"* manner, rambling on with empty phrases, as Jesus warned in His introduction to the Lord's prayer: ***"use not vain repetitions, as the heathen do"*** (Matthew 6:7).

> "Prayer is to come first and foremost, not from our head but from our heart."

🔍 Something to think about...

- How do you know that it is not presumption for you to approach such a great and holy God when you are so insignificant as a creature, and so sinful as a sinner?
- Why is it no excuse for neglecting prayer that we are not sure how to pray?
- Is there a difference between *"repetition"* and *"vain repetition"* in prayer?

How should we approach God in prayer?

The Lord's prayer begins, "Our Father, which art in heaven." These words form the preface, or introduction, to the Lord's prayer, and they teach us several things.

💬 What doth the preface of the Lord's prayer teach us?

A. The preface of the Lord's prayer (which is, "Our Father which art in heaven"), teacheth us to draw near to God with all holy reverence and confidence, as children to a father, able and ready to help us; and that we should pray with and for others.

We are encouraged by the preface

(a) We are encouraged to draw near to God with reverence and confidence
The preface to the Lord's prayer directs us to call on God as our Father who is in heaven. We are therefore to come with the utmost respect, not casually and frivolously, because God is in heaven, holy and exalted, and we are on earth, sinners and needy. Yet at the same time we are not to come apprehensively or reluctantly, but with full confidence in God because He is our Father. A father with grown up children was reminiscing about when his children were very little, and how his daughter brought him her damaged toy with the request, *"Daddy, fix it!"* Those who are God's children, knowing that He is the holy and glorious Lord, can nevertheless come to Him the way that little children come to their father, completely certain that he will have time for them and take an interest in their problems and be able to fix things for them.

> "God our Father is ready to help us."

(b) We are encouraged to draw near to God as a Father who is able and ready to help us

1. God our Father is **"able to ... help us."** Sometimes our natural father is unable to help us; perhaps when we need him he is not close to hand. This Father is never unable to help His children. All His power and all His kindness is at the ready to meet the needs of His children.
2. God our Father is **"ready to help us."** For many different reasons our natural fathers are not always willing to hear. This Father has His ear open to the cry of His children and is never too busy or pre-occupied. We see from Psalm 103 how tenderly the Lord cares for His children. **"Such pity as a father hath / unto his children dear; / like pity shows the Lord to such / as worship him in fear"** (v13 metrical). In Matthew 7:7-11 the

Lord Jesus asks the people whether a good father would give his son a stone instead of bread, or a snake instead of a fish. The answer, of course, is that no good father would ever do such a thing. The Lord then says that if we who are sinners would not do that, surely we can be confident that the Lord, who is good, would never give anything bad or hurtful to His children.

> "We do not need to be praying audibly in order to pray with others."

(c) We are encouraged to **pray with and for others**

The Lord taught His disciples to pray, not *"my Father,"* but, *"our Father."* This shows us that we should frequently pray *"with and for others"* as well as by and for ourselves individually.

- **We are to pray jointly with other people,** whether in the formal assemblies of God's people, or at home in our families, or between our friends, sympathetically asking God to meet their needs and thanking God with them for their blessings. We do not need to be praying audibly in order to pray with others. For example, when the minister is praying in a church service, we should think of ourselves as praying with him and with the others present, because he should be praying for things that are appropriate for all of us. This is also why the minister and anyone who prays aloud in public services should frame their requests as coming not from themselves as individuals, "Lord, I pray...", but on behalf of all who are gathered, "Lord, we pray..."
- **We are also to pray for other people.** When we seek spiritual and providential blessings for ourselves, we should also wish them for others, whether they are close to us, or the Lord's people, or people in authority, or even our enemies.

Q Something to think about...

Personal reflection
When you begin your prayers, *"our Father,"* do you know for yourself the Father it speaks of, not just in the general sense that He is your Creator, but in the particular sense that He has adopted you into the family of His saved children?

- How often do you pray with other people? Does it count if someone else is praying and you only listen?
- How often do you pray for other people?

How should we reverence God in prayer?

Question 101 turns to the first petition in the Lord's prayer. A petition is a request, something we ask for. There are six petitions in the Lord's prayer, and the first is, 'Hallowed be thy name.' One way of analysing the relationship between the six petitions is to see the first petition as the main one, and the remaining five petitions as ways of fulfilling it. Another way of analysing them is to take the first three petitions as referring to God and the remaining three petitions as referring to ourselves and our neighbours. In either case, the position which this petition has at the very beginning of the prayer tells us that this is a very important thing to ask for.

> **💬** What do we pray for in the first petition?
>
> A. In the first petition (which is, "Hallowed be thy name"), we pray, that God would enable us and others to glorify him in all that whereby he maketh himself known; and that he would dispose all things to his own glory.

What is the first petition about?

This petition is about the name of the Lord. The Catechism explains that what it means by God's name is *"all that whereby He maketh Himself known."* As we have already seen from Questions 53 to 56, this includes:

* The names and titles of God, such as *"God, Jehovah, Lord of Hosts"*
* God's ordinances, including His Word
* God's works of creation, providence, and redemption

The first petition is therefore concerned with the widest possible picture God gives of Himself in all the ways by which He makes Himself known to us.

What does the first petition ask for?

"We cannot add anything to His glory."

The petition asks that the name of the Lord would be *"hallowed."* To hallow something means to honour it, and especially to honour it as holy. The equivalent term used in the Catechism is that God's name would be *'glorified.'* Of course, God's name is already utterly glorious. We cannot add anything to His glory. This petition asks for God to be known and honoured, by us and others, for the glorious God that He is. We are directed in Psalm 96:8 (metrical version): *"Give ye the glory to the Lord / that to his name is due."* How can this be done in practice? What exactly are we asking the Lord to do in this petition?

(a) We are asking that we would **be enabled to glorify Him**

- We are confessing that we are unable to glorify Him without the enabling of the Holy Spirit. Glorifying God is part of our *'chief end,'* and here we are asking for help to do what it is our chief purpose to do.
- We are asking for help to know the Lord as He has revealed Himself to us; pondering His names, titles, attributes, and works in a reverent and worshipful way.
- We are asking for help to forsake our sins, which rob Him of His glory.
- We are asking for help to live believing and obedient lives to His honour.

What we ask for ourselves in this petition also applies to all those round about us and to the whole of humanity. We are also asking:

- To be enabled to do all that we can, to see that others also grow in knowledge of God as He has revealed Himself to us. ***"Extol the Lord with me, let us / exalt his name together"*** (Psalm 34:3, metrical version).
- For help to promote the honour of God in society and to oppose all that is dishonouring to God, whether bad laws or wicked practices.
- For others to be brought to know the Lord and honour Him as they should.

(b) We ask God to **honour His own name**

We are seeking in this petition that the Lord would ***"dispose all things,"*** or arrange all things, to His own glory. We are asking Him to work in the world in such a way that His name would be honoured. Now we know from our Bibles that the Lord is very concerned to do just that. Sometimes you will hear someone say that they do not wish to do a certain thing in case they lose or spoil their good name as a result. In a far higher way this is also true of God. He always acts to honour His own great name. This means that in this petition we are not asking the Lord to do something that He might not do or is in any way reluctant to do. We are asking Him to do what He is most willing to do.

- We pray that He would use all the different events in the world, which occur, of course, according to His own will, as means to hallow His name, even those events which seem, at first, to do the very opposite.
- We pray that He would use His creation to impress people with His power and Godhead.
- We pray that He would use His Word to prevent and remove atheism and wrong ideas of who He is.
- We pray that He would use His work of redemption to save people and enable them to glorify Him.

> "He always acts to honour His own great name."

🔍 Something to think about...

• In Psalm 67, the psalmist asks God to bless us by making His salvation known in the earth. Which part of this petition of the Lord's prayer does this psalm expand on? How many different ways does the psalmist express this desire in Psalm 67?

Personal reflection
When you pray, do you make it your first priority that you would glorify God?

How should we pray for God's kingdom?

Two kings are at war with each other, and neither will rest until the other is destroyed. One king is Satan. The other king is Christ, who the Father has appointed to reign. Although the Catechism mentions the kingdoms of grace and glory, these are really only two aspects of God's one kingdom. Satan and Christ are implacably opposed, so that to support the one automatically means wishing the destruction of the other. We will follow the Catechism in looking at the opposing kingdoms, praying for the Father's kingdom to come.

💬 What do we pray for in the second petition?

A. In the second petition (which is, "Thy kingdom come"), we pray, That Satan's kingdom may be destroyed; and that the kingdom of grace may be advanced, ourselves and others brought into it, and kept in it; and that the kingdom of glory may be hastened.

Satan's kingdom

"When we pray, 'Thy kingdom come,' we are praying for the downfall and destruction of Satan and an end to wickedness and evil."

The kingdom of Satan is the sum total of everything in the universe which is contrary to God. Satan is called the ***"prince of this world"*** (John 14:30). However, Satan does not have control of everything that happens in the world. God rules over everything, including Satan. Satan has no right to rule, because he got his kingdom through wickedness, when he deceived Adam and Eve. God now permits him to reign in his evil kingdom the way that a gaoler keeps his prisoners captive.

When we pray, ***"Thy kingdom come,"*** we are praying for the downfall and destruction of Satan and an end to wickedness and evil. Satan's kingdom is populated by devils and rebellious sinners. In this petition we are praying for God's enemies, either to be subdued by His grace or destroyed where they persist in hating God and Christ and God's people. We are praying for the Lord Jesus Christ to overthrow the kingdom and work of Satan, banishing Satan, his angels and all who do not repent, to hell forever.

Christ's kingdom

The kingdom of grace

The Father has appointed the Lord Jesus Christ to rule His kingdom. The Jews hoped that when Christ came He would set up His kingdom in Jerusalem and reign there as king. However, Christ made it very clear that His kingdom was not that sort of kingdom. It is a spiritual kingdom, populated by His people who were all once rebels in Satan's kingdom, but who have been made willing by the Spirit's power to have Christ as their new king. It is called a *"kingdom of grace"* because it is only by the Spirit's grace and mercy that anyone is brought into it, their sins being pardoned and their lives changed.

When we pray, *"Thy kingdom come,"* we are praying *"that the kingdom of grace may be advanced,"* that is, for the progress of Christ's work in this world. We are praying for the gospel to become known in parts of the world where it is unknown, for the Jews to be converted and for the fullness of the Gentiles to be brought in. We are praying for the gospel to be better known where it is already known, through the gospel being preached more accurately and effectively, and Christ's people living more holy lives.

We are also praying for *"ourselves and others to be brought in"* to Christ's kingdom. How can that happen? There is only one way: *"Except a man be born again, he cannot see the kingdom of God"* (John 3:3). We are praying for our own conversion and the conversion of others, praying that we will be delivered from the power of darkness and taken into the kingdom of Christ (Colossians 1:13).

We are also praying for *"ourselves and others…[to be] kept"* in Christ's kingdom. We also pray for civil governments to acknowledge and practically support the Church in its work. Satan is constantly trying to undermine Christ's kingdom and destroy those who are in it. The children of the Father who belong to His kingdom are also still sinners, and unable to keep themselves in the kingdom of grace. So we need to pray for keeping for ourselves and others, both in the sense that we will be enabled to live consistently godly lives, and in the sense that we will eventually be taken into the kingdom of glory.

The kingdom of glory

The *"kingdom of glory"* is the complete and perfect fulfilment of the *"kingdom of grace."* These are not two separate kingdoms but the beginning and the completion of one and the same kingdom. All the children of the Father will be made perfectly blessed in the full enjoying of God to all eternity, and Christ will be made all and in all. It is true that Christ has already defeated Satan and all the works of darkness (John 12:31, Colossians 2:15). However, not until Christ's second coming will Satan's work be utterly ended. Then the kingdom of glory will be seen in all its perfection and triumph.

> "All the children of the Father will be made perfectly blessed in the full enjoying of God to all eternity, and Christ will be made all and in all."

When we pray, *"Thy kingdom come,"* we are praying *"that the kingdom of glory may be hastened."* Of course, God has already fixed the time when Christ will come again. We are not praying that this time would be changed, but we are expressing how eagerly we are looking forward to it. When an engaged couple set their wedding date, they know it is still a long time away in the future, yet they feel it can't come soon enough. We pray, ***"Come quickly, Lord Jesus"*** (Revelation 22:20), because we can't wait for all the promised blessings of grace to come in this life. We also long to be with Him and to see Him face to face and to be made perfectly free from sin.

Q Something to think about...

Personal reflection

Who is your king? What kingdom are you a part of? Are you campaigning on Christ's side or Satan's side? Do you really wish for Christ's kingdom to come and all His enemies to be destroyed?

If you are not converted, do you pray for your own conversion? Do you pray for other people to be converted too?

Do you share the longing for the kingdom of glory to come as quickly as possible?

How should we pray about God's will?

After praying for God's name to be glorified and God's kingdom to come, we move on in the third petition to pray for God's will to be done.

---

103 What do we pray for in the third petition?

A. In the third petition (which is, "Thy will be done in earth, as it is in heaven"), we pray, That God, by his grace, would make us able and willing to know, obey and submit to his will in all things, as the angels do in heaven.

God's **will**

God's will is what He wishes to do. He has given us His *revealed* will in His Word, which is to be the rule of our lives. He also has His *secret* will, by which He has foreordained everything that comes to pass. We are unable to know His secret will, except in the little that we see of it as it unfolds in His mysterious providence, and as He has outlined it in the

> "He also has His secret will, by which He has foreordained everything that comes to pass."

prophecies of the Bible. In this petition, the focus is on God's revealed will, as we cannot pray to know God's secret will, although this petition includes the idea that we should pray for submission to God's secret will as well as His revealed will.

God's **will in heaven**

In heaven God's will is always perfectly obeyed. There is never a point in heaven when obedience is less fully or gladly given than at any other time. It is the delight of heaven and all who are there to obey the Lord's will. According to the Larger Catechism, in heaven God's will is done with *"humility, cheerfulness, faithfulness, diligence, zeal, sincerity, and constancy"* (Larger Catechism Q192). When we pray, *"Thy will be done as it is in heaven,"* we are praying for these things to characterise us as we seek to obey God.

God's **will on earth**

Of course there is a great difference between heaven and earth. There is an obstacle to obedience here which is absent in heaven, because in this world sin is present. Before sin was present the will of God was done on earth as in heaven. When sin came, that was completely changed, and disobedience and hatred to God's will came in. Because of this we need to seek the Lord's help to do His will.

(a) We are praying for help **to know God's will**

As sinners we do not have a proper understanding of God's will. Before we can ever begin to obey the Lord we have to be made *"able and willing to know"* what the will of God is. When we pray, *"Thy will be done,"* we are like the psalmist in Psalm 119 when he asks the Lord to open his eyes, or understanding, in order for him to see the will of the Lord as revealed in His Word (verse 18). In Colossians 1:9 Paul prays that the Christians at Colosse would come to an ever-increasing understanding of the Lord's will, *"that ye might be filled with the knowledge of his will in all wisdom and spiritual understanding."*

(b) We are praying for help **to obey God's will**

Not only are we ignorant as far as God's will is concerned but we are inclined to do the very opposite of what God wants (Romans 8:7). When we pray, *"Thy will be done,"* we are praying to be made able and willing to do His will. The Bible is full of encouragement to believe that God is able and willing to teach us. God promises in Ezekiel, *"A new heart also will I give you, and a new spirit will I put within you.....I will put my spirit within you, and cause you to walk in my statutes, and ye shall keep my judgments and do them"* (36:26-27). Paul writing to the Philippians speaks of God as the one that *"worketh in you both to will and to do of his good pleasure"* (2:13).

(c) We are praying for help **to submit to God's will**

As the plan of God for our lives unfolds, there will be many things which we do not like, and many matters which we wish were different to the way they are. We may suffer problems, illness, bereavement, disappointment and persecution. At such times it is very hard to submit to God's will. It can be hard, even for the mature Christian, to see how the plan of God can possibly be a perfect plan. But when we pray, *"Thy will be done,"* we are praying that in the middle of all our difficulties we will be able to submit to God's will. Job's wife told him that he might as well *"curse God and die"* because of all his difficulties. Job answered, *"What? Shall we receive good at the hand of God, and shall we not receive evil?"* (Job 2:9-10) Job was demonstrating the attitude that we are asking for when we pray, *"Thy will be done."*

> "Before sin was present the will of God was done on earth as in heaven."

🔍 Something to think about...

- Why do you need God's grace to make you *able* to know, obey, and submit to His will?
- Why do you need God's grace to make you *willing* to know, obey, and submit to His will?

How should we pray about our earthly needs?

Perhaps all of us are guilty of focussing on the needs of our daily lives in a way that puts these needs, real as they are, in the very first place in our prayers and thinking. But out of the six petitions in the Lord's prayer only one refers to our earthly needs and it is not the first but the fourth of these petitions. That should remind us that the way God wants us to prioritise our lives is by putting Him (His name, His kingdom, and His will) ahead of our earthly needs.

At the same time the inclusion of this petition for daily bread reminds us that our earthly needs are not to be disregarded and they are not unimportant in the sight of God.

💬 What do we pray for in the fourth petition?

A. In the fourth petition (which is, "Give us this day our daily bread"), we pray, That of God's free gift we may receive a competent portion of the good things of this life, and enjoy his blessing with them.

Universal needs

> "Whatever we have, it comes from God as a free gift."

The word **"bread"** in this petition includes all the food which we need.

It is also a way of speaking about everything that we need in order to live in this world. It includes food and drink, housing, clothing, income, health, medicine, air for breathing, and everything necessary for our comfort and convenience. It includes everything we need when we are awake and when we are asleep. It includes everything we need for the whole of our lives. The Catechism summarises all this as, **"the good things of this life."**

When we pray, **"Give us this day our daily bread,"** we are confessing that by our sin we have forfeited our right to even the basic necessities of life, and acknowledging that we have no control over our own circumstances to ensure that we get what we need.

Universal Provider

We are so needy. But the Lord's children can go to the Lord Himself, appealing to Him as their Father in heaven. He who provides for all people at all times and in all places, takes special care that His children are well supplied with what they need.

"God knows best what each person needs, and He sees that for most people, a competent portion does not include dazzling wealth and an extravagant lifestyle."

It is a free provision

Whatever we have, it comes from God as a free gift. God is sovereign in what He gives and who He gives it to. When we pray, *"Give,"* we are humbly asking that He would look kindly on us and give us what we need. If He does mercifully give us what we need we are to be thankful. We are to remember that we deserve nothing and that He could rightly leave us with nothing.

It is a daily provision

Remember when the children of Israel were in the desert and collected manna each morning except the Sabbath? This kept them constantly dependent on the Lord and it was a guard against thinking that they could manage without Him. We are all inclined to think we can fend for ourselves or that things will somehow work out for us by themselves. When we pray, *"Give us this day,"* we are asking for the things we need at the moment. If we use the wording of the equivalent petition in Luke, *"Give us day by day,"* we are asking for the things we need repeatedly. We are dependent on the Lord to supply all our needs, right now and continually. We should pray like Agur, who specifically asked that the Lord would not give him so much that he would be full and deny Him (Proverbs 30:8-9). If we received all we need in one big lump sum we would be inclined to forget all about God who had given it to us.

It is a competent provision

We are praying for bread, not for caviar and luxury yachts. We are asking for just what is *"competent,"* or appropriate and adequate, the things which will allow us to survive and live comfortably. When we pray for *"our daily bread,"* we are asking, like Agur, *"Give me neither poverty nor riches; feed me with food convenient for me"* (Proverbs 30:8). God knows best what each person needs, and He sees that for most people, a competent portion does not include dazzling wealth and an extravagant lifestyle. We are praying that our idea of what we need would be aligned with God's, so that we would be happy with whatever He gives us, knowing that it is suited to our own real needs in God's view.

It is an incomplete provision without the Father's blessing

Our possession of the good things of this life is only part of the answer to this petition. We also need *"His blessing with them."* God meets the earthly needs of all sorts of people, from those who commit dreadful atrocities to angry atheists to people who have never so much as heard of Jesus. He sends rain so that the harvest can be enjoyed both by the just and the unjust. We all have our portion of the good things of this life by God's free gift. But we need God to bless them to us so that we would benefit by them, make good use of them, and use them to His glory.

🔍 Something to think about...

- When you compare yourself to others, would you say you have a competent portion of the good things of this life, or more than a competent portion, or less than a competent portion?
- What needs do you have right now which you need to pray for **"this day?"** What needs do you have recurrently which you need to pray for **"day by day?"** Thinking over the past few weeks, what are some of the ways that God has provided for these various needs? How has He added His blessing to them?
- The story is told of a woman sitting at a table with very little food in front of her, who thanked the Lord with the words, **"All this, and Jesus Christ too!"** How does this illustrate the attitude you should have towards (a) what you have and (b) the relative importance of temporal and spiritual blessings?

How should we pray about our sins?

If the fourth petition was about our daily bread, the fifth petition is about our daily debt. Every day we need to ask our Father to meet not only our earthly needs but also our spiritual needs.

105. What do we pray for in the fifth petition?

A. In the fifth petition (which is, "And forgive us our debts, as we forgive our debtors"), we pray, That God, for Christ's sake, would freely pardon all our sins; which we are the rather encouraged to ask, because by his grace we are enabled from the heart to forgive others.

Our debts

(a) We are debtors

I When someone buys something with the promise of paying later, or when someone borrows money from a friend or the bank, they are going into debt, and they remain a debtor until they pay back what they owe. Lending and borrowing money between individuals and businesses is not necessarily

"Every time we sin ... we are running up more debt on our accounts with God."

sinful. However, what we owe to God is spiritual rather than commercial. We owe God two kinds of things. One is obedience to His law. The other is making amends for breaking His law. Every time we sin and fail to make amends, we are running up more debt on our accounts with God. We have the debt of original sin and committed sins; sins of omission and sins of commission; sins of thought, word, and action; sins of weakness and wilful sins; secret sins and open sins; sins against God, sins against our neighbour, and sins against ourselves. When we pray, **"Forgive us our debts,"** we are confessing all this guilt and our inability to make any satisfaction to God for it.

(b) Our debts can be paid

Like all our monetary debts, these spiritual debts have to be paid. But we are utterly unable to pay this debt. We arrive into the world already spiritually bankrupt, and all we do is accumulate more and more spiritual debt as we continue to sin. We have no spiritual resources to hand which we can put towards paying off our debt, nor any spiritual skills that we can use in spiritual employment to earn spiritual capital. When we pray, **"Forgive us our debts,"** we are not praying that we would be able to pay our debts. Instead, we are praying **"that God would freely pardon all our sins," "for Christ's sake."** Christ obeyed the law perfectly on behalf of His people and paid the full penalty for their disobedience. Since Christ has settled the debt, God freely pardons all our sins. As we pray for daily provision, so we are praying for daily pardon for our present and continual failings, and daily more assurance of God's forgiveness.

"Our attitude to others ought to reflect God's attitude to us."

Our debtors

(a) We have debtors

We are in daily contact with one another. The things we say and do have an effect on those who are around us. Living as we do in a fallen world, populated by fallen creatures like ourselves, these effects are frequently bad effects. We do wrong to one another and accumulate sinful debts not only with God but also with each other. People become each other's debtors by wronging each other.

(b) We forgive our debtors

We tend to be disinclined to pardon those who have wronged us, even when we are inclined to seek pardon for ourselves. We tend to judge the sins of others against us far more harshly than we judge our sins against God. We grudge forgiving others.

It is common to hear people say, *'I can never forgive that person for what they did.'* Sometimes this is what we say ourselves, or at least it is our attitude. But how can we expect God to forgive us our debts if we refuse to forgive our debtors? Is it not shocking and shameful to expect pardon from God while we refuse to give it to others? Can we really expect God to ignore such inconsistency? John Wesley once heard a man say that he would never forgive his servant for theft, *'for,'* said the man, *'I never forgive.'* Wesley replied, *'In that case I hope you never sin.'*

However, the Christian, by God's grace, is enabled to forgive others for the wrong they have done them, and indeed to forgive them from the heart. Our attitude to others ought to reflect God's attitude to us. Those who have been freely pardoned should reflect God's wonderful forgiveness in their dealings with others.

When we pray, *"Forgive us ... as we forgive our debtors,"* our forgiveness of others is not a motive to God to forgive us, but it is an encouragement to us to ask forgiveness for ourselves from God. If we cannot honestly pray, *"as we forgive our debtors,"* then we must seek this forgiving spirit as surely as we must seek pardon for our sin.

🔍 Something to think about...

- Have your spiritual debts been paid off or are you still deep in debt to God?
- If you have had your spiritual debts paid, is that obvious in your dealings with others or would you like them to stay deep in debt?

How should we pray about temptation?

Every day we need our Father to provide our bread and our forgiveness, and every day we need our Father to keep us safe from our own sin. In the sixth petition, now that we have prayed for daily provision and daily pardon, we come to pray for daily protection.

💬 What do we pray for in the sixth petition?

A. In the sixth petition (which is, "And lead us not into temptation, but deliver us from evil"), we pray, That God would either keep us from being tempted to sin, or support and deliver us when we are tempted.

A humble request

This is a request from someone who is not self-confident, but feels very much their own weakness as far as sin and temptation is concerned. When we pray, *"Lead us not into temptation, but deliver us from evil,"* we are making several humble acknowledgements.

> "Not only are we very vulnerable to temptations, but we are very prone to expose ourselves to temptation."

We are humbly acknowledging that God is sovereign when He allows temptations
In God's providence, circumstances may arise which are not sinful in themselves but which provoke us to sin. For example, we may fall into the sin of pride when we get a promotion at work. God also sometimes allows Satan to use his trickery and his fierceness to draw us into sin.

We are humbly acknowledging our situation is dangerous
We live in a sinful world with a sinful heart, and with a sinful tempter who is always prowling about like *"a roaring lion ... seeking whom he may devour"* (1 Peter 5:8).

We are humbly acknowledging our inability to cope with temptations
Not only are we very vulnerable to temptations, but we are very prone to expose ourselves to temptation. The Apostle Peter boasted that he would never forsake Jesus. He was not concerned about temptation coming because he was certain that he would be well able to stand firm when it came, but in this he did not take account of his own inability.

A hopeful request

When we pray, *"Lead us not into temptation, but deliver us from evil,"* we are expressing our hope and confidence that the Lord is able to either keep us from being tempted in the first place, or to *"support and deliver us when we are tempted."*

We are asking the Lord to **keep temptation at bay**
The Lord can order our circumstances and lives in such a way that we are delivered from temptation. He controls the events that happen, the activities of the devil, the attractions of the world, and the inclinations of our heart. He is able to strengthen our graces and make the means of grace effective for our souls.

We are asking the Lord to **deliver us out of evil**
When we do fall into temptation, the Lord is able to support us (so that we don't fall as deeply into sin as we might) and to deliver us (by recovering us out of the sin we have fallen into). *"God is faithful, who will not suffer you to be tempted above that ye are able; but will with the temptation also make a way to escape, that ye may be able to bear it"* (1 Corinthians 10:13). Peter tells us that the Lord knows how to *"deliver the godly out of temptations"* (2 Peter 2:9).

> "God has a good and wise purpose behind it when He brings His people into situations where they will be tempted."

We are asking the Lord to **bring good out of evil**
God has a good and wise purpose behind it when He brings His people into situations where they will be tempted. Such circumstances test their faith and obedience and they can be a means of strengthening the believer, as, by grace, they overcome Satan and sin. Under temptation the believer also discovers their own weakness, and so comes to rely more directly on the Lord's strength in a way that they would not have done otherwise.

We are asking the Lord **for ultimate deliverance from all temptation and evil**
This petition looks forward to the time when the believer will be completely delivered from sin, when the Lord brings them to heaven. Although this petition is answered increasingly in this life, as the believer grows more and more in holiness, it will only be fully answered when the believer is taken to glory.

Q Something to think about...

- Believers sometimes fall into temptation in the very area where they are most marked for grace. Peter thought he was completely committed to the Saviour, and then he denied Him. Elijah showed tremendous courage on Mount Carmel, and then gave way to paralysing fear and depression. Has this ever happened to you? How does it reinforce the need to pray, *"Lead us not into temptation"*?
- How did the Lord support and deliver Job when Job's endurance was tested? How did the Lord support and deliver Jonah when Jonah disobeyed his commission?

Personal reflection
When you pray this petition, does it reflect a real fear of your own sinful weakness and the bitterness of falling into temptation? Or would you really rather have more opportunities to sin and your main concern is to be delivered from the unpleasant consequences of sinning?

How should we close our prayers?

It would be completely mistaken to think that these last few words do not matter very much in the Lord's prayer, as if they were just there as a way of closing the prayer after all the important things had been said. In fact the conclusion of the Lord's prayer teaches us at least three significant things.

What doth the conclusion of the Lord's prayer teach us?

A. The conclusion of the Lord's prayer (which is, "For Thine is the kingdom, and the power, and the glory, for ever, Amen") teacheth us to take our encouragement in prayer from God only, and in our prayers to praise him, ascribing kingdom, power, and glory to him. And, in testimony of our desire, and assurance to be heard, we say, Amen.

We should have **encouragement in prayer**

"To Him belongs the kingdom, the power, and the glory."

There is plenty to discourage us from praying: from our own sense of sin to our consciousness of what big requests we are making. But the conclusion of the Lord's prayer teaches us that we should be encouraged when we pray.

- We are encouraged to find reasons to pray. We can take each of the petitions individually and reinforce them with the reason, *"For thine is the kingdom, and the power, and the glory."* *"Give us this day our daily bread,... for thine is the kingdom..."* *"Lead us not into temptation,... for thine is the kingdom..."* Clearly these reasons do not carry any weight to persuade God to do things for us. Instead they are reasons which should energise our praying and increase our faith in God.
- Our encouragement in prayer comes *"from God only."* Of course we would be discouraged if we looked at ourselves or our circumstances; but instead we look at God. Daniel focused on the mercy of God and the honour of God: *"We do not present our supplications before thee for our righteousnesses, but for thy great mercies ... O Lord, hearken and do; defer not, for thine own sake, O my God"* (Daniel 9:18-19). Asa focused on God's omnipotence, His faithfulness, and His name: *"Lord, it is nothing with thee to help, whether with many, or with them that have no power: help us, O Lord our God; for we rest on thee, and in thy name we go..."* (2 Chronicles 14:11)

We should have **praise in prayer**

Our prayers should not be just a list of requests. We should also remember to praise God when we pray to Him, acknowledging that to Him belongs the kingdom, the power, and the glory.

(a) "Thine is the kingdom"

Our Father is a king. God, the Father of His people, is supreme. He **"does according to his will in the army of heaven and amongst the inhabitants of the earth"** (Daniel 4:35). He will withhold nothing that is good for His children, whether in nature or in grace, because both the kingdom of nature and the kingdom of grace belong to Him.

(b) "Thine is ... the power"

Some kings are not very powerful and no earthly king is all-powerful. However the king to whom we come in prayer, our Father in heaven, is all-powerful; He rules and governs over all the nations of the world. This means that He is able to meet all our needs and keep all His promises. We may be praying and feeling very discouraged about it all. We may well feel so small and insignificant that there is little hope of our prayers ever seeing an answer. But we should take courage. Our hope lies in the fact that the Lord is a powerful king. No difficulty whatever will get in the way of His promises being fulfilled.

(c) "Thine is ... the glory"

God possesses all possible excellencies. He is glorious in Himself and as He makes Himself known. All that He intends and promises to do (and everything that we are licensed to ask Him for) will bring honour and glory to Him.

(d) "For ever"

Unlike earthly rulers, who come and go, the Lord who is our Father will never cease to rule; the glory, power and kingdom are His forever. From eternity to eternity, He is always glorious, omnipotent, and majestic.

> "Our Father in heaven is all-powerful; He rules and governs over all the nations of the world."

We should have **desire and assurance in prayer**

"Amen" is a Hebrew word which conveys the idea of truth and certainty, and is used to express someone's agreement with what is being said. It was the word Jesus used in His statements beginning, **"Verily, verily,"** or **"Truly, truly."** When it is used at the end of a prayer, it means, **'Let it be so!'** or, **'So it shall be!'**

When we say, **"Amen,"** we testify our desire that we really do wish for the things we have asked for. We long for the Lord to do as He has said. The things agreeable to His will are also the things agreeable to our will. **"Amen, so let it be!"** (Psalm 72:19, metrical).

When we say, **"Amen,"** we also testify our assurance and certainty that God really will answer our requests. He is both willing and able to help us. He is both willing and able to do everything He has purposed and promised to do. **'Amen, so shall it be!'**

217

🔍 Something to think about...

- When Daniel wanted forgiveness, he appealed to God's mercy. When Asa wanted help, he appealed to God's omnipotence. How does the thought of God's various different attributes help you to tailor your specific petitions and gain confidence in God to answer these petitions?
- Why should we join praises with our prayers?

Personal reflection

When you say *"Amen"* at the conclusion of your prayers, does it signal a real desire that your requests would be granted when they are agreeable to God's will? Does it signal a real certainty that God will do everything that He has promised to do?